This coloring book belongs to:

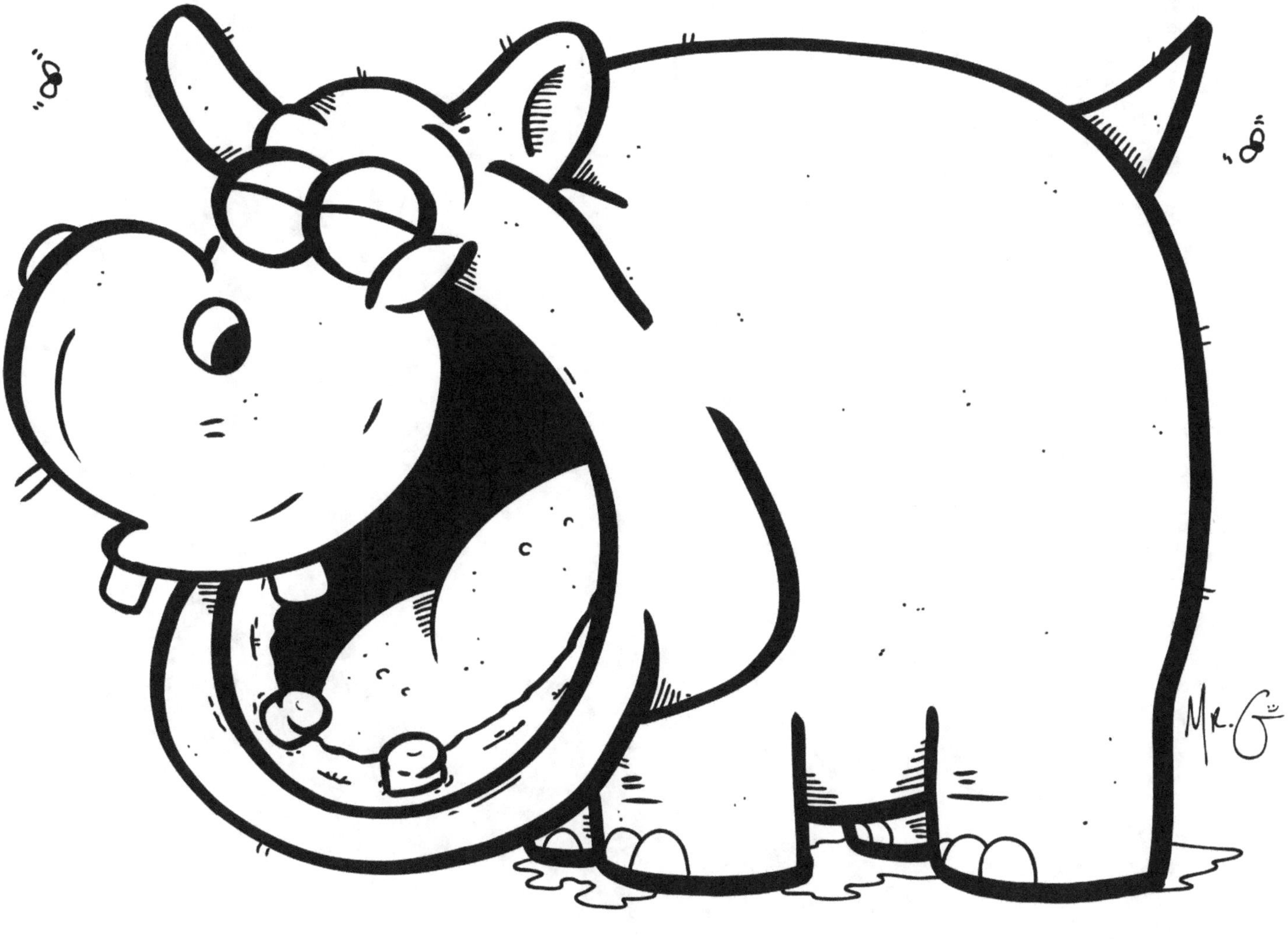

The Animals & Friends Coloring Book

(Volume One)

Illustrated By

Mr. Gray

Dedicated

to my nieces and nephews: Brooke, Vaughn,
Landon & Alexa. No matter where you go,
my doodles will always be with you.
Happy Coloring!

WELCOME

to The Animals & Friends Coloring Book Volume One!

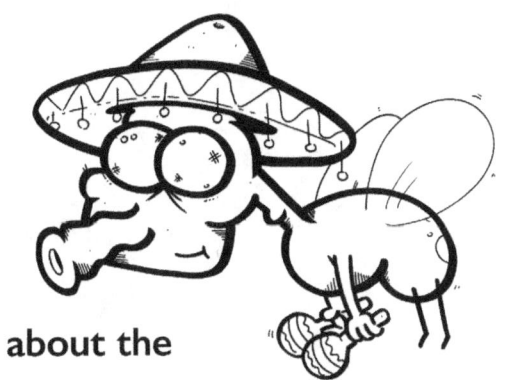

What's Inside?

1. FUN FACTS:

Each page has a fun and interesting factoid about the animal, insect or creature!

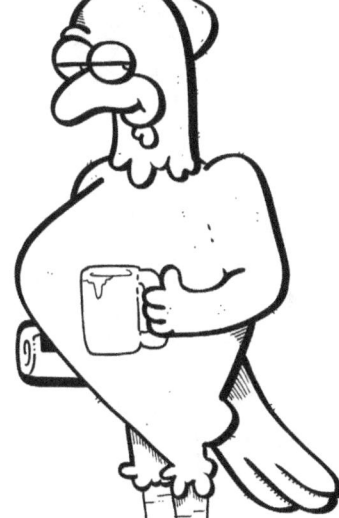

2. HIDDEN TREASURE:

Mr. Gray hid **8** super secret items in this coloring book! Can you find them all?

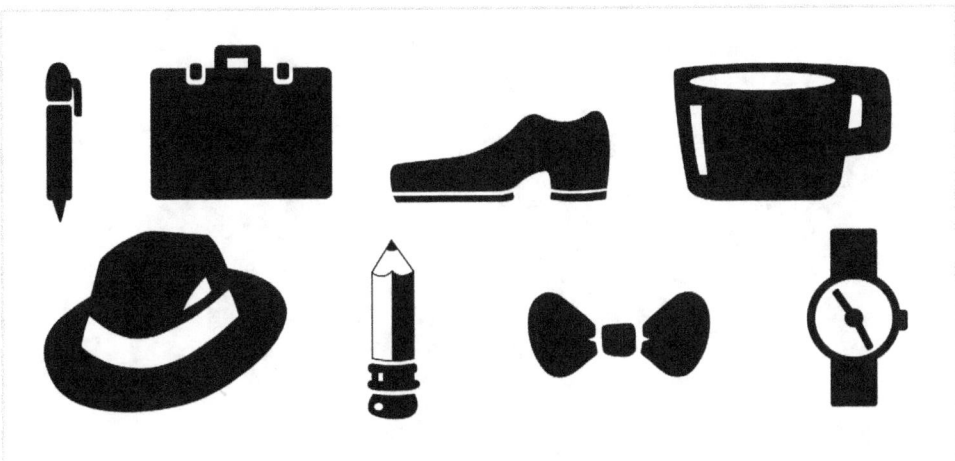

* The answer sheet can be found in back of the coloring book.

3. ONE-SIDED:

Each coloring page is printed on one side so you have the option to display your masterpiece and to color it with your favorite markers.

* *TIP: Put a piece of paper behind the page you're coloring to prevent bleeding.*

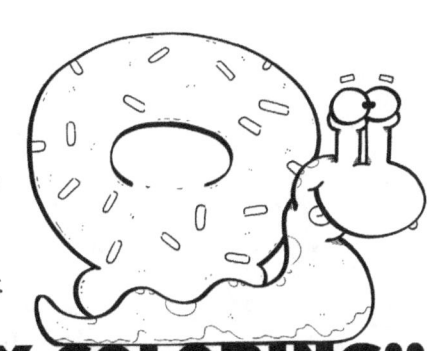

HAPPY COLORING!!

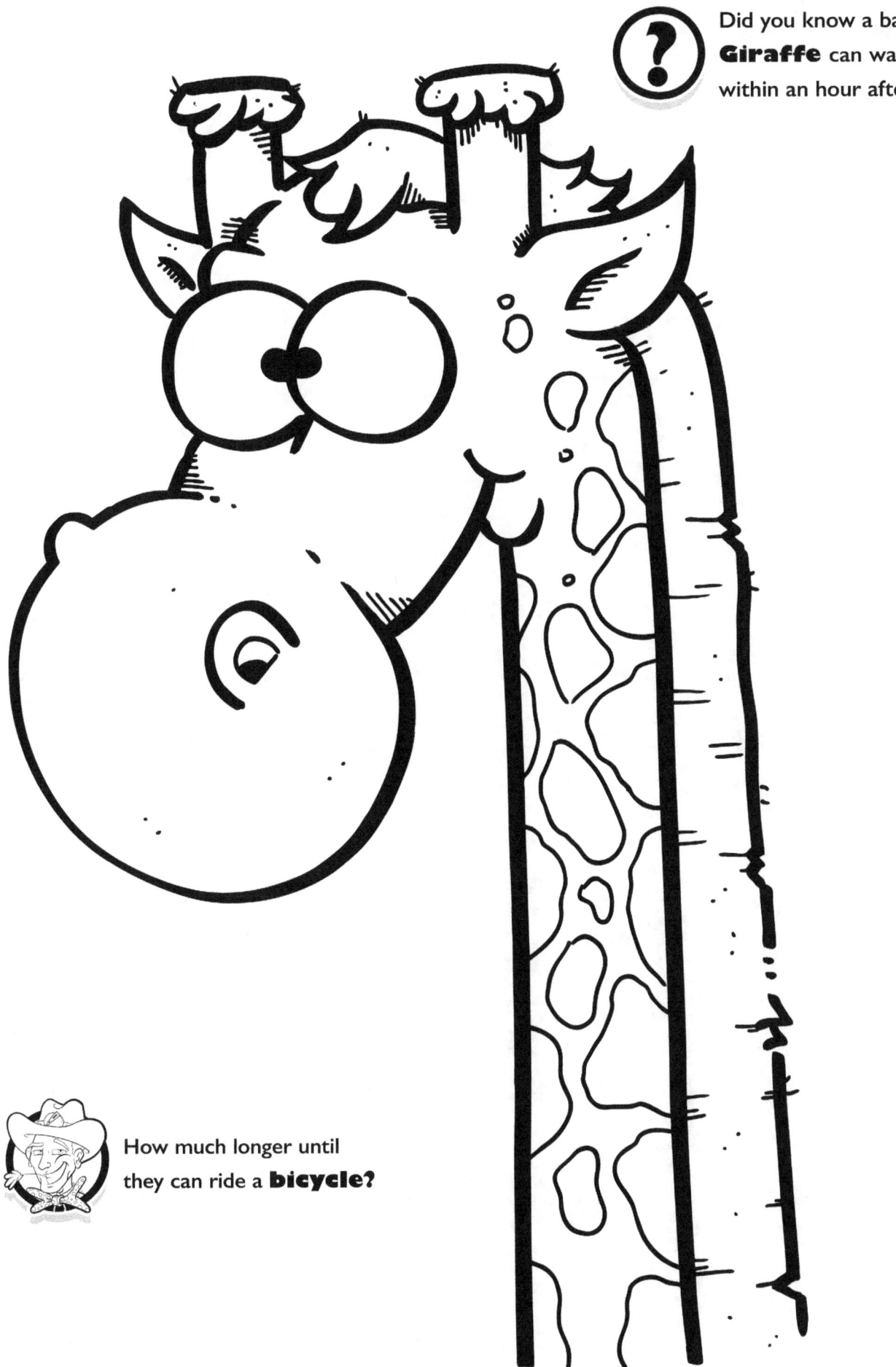

Did you know a baby **Giraffe** can walk within an hour after birth?

How much longer until they can ride a **bicycle?**

Did you know **Beavers** use their broad tails like rudders to steer through the water like a boat?

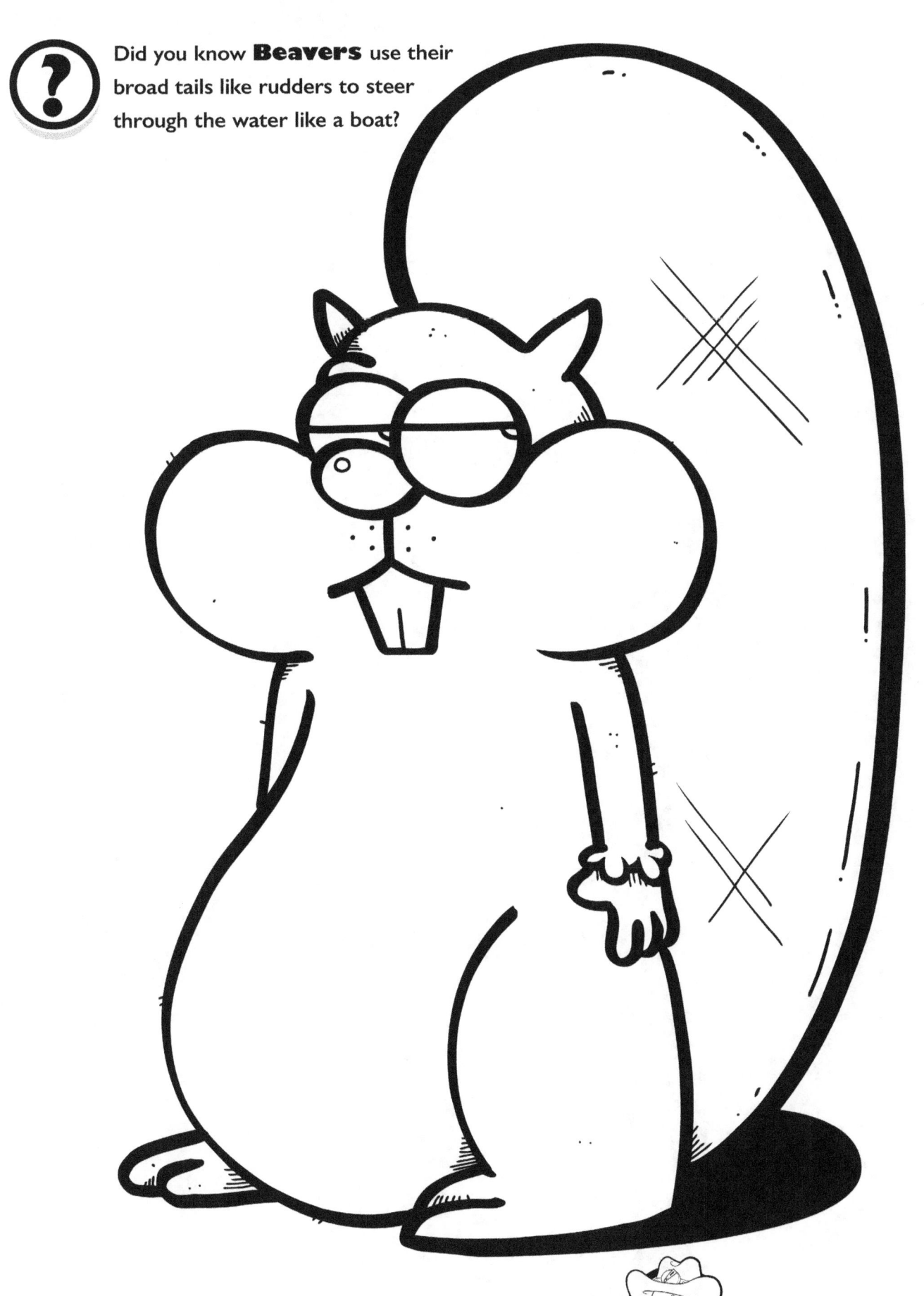

Ahoy! The **S.S. Beaver!**

? Did you know the largest crab in the world is the **Japanese Spider Crab?** And the best part, some measure up to 13 feet across!

I know what I'm **having for dinner.**

 Did you know that **Snakes** smell with their tongue?

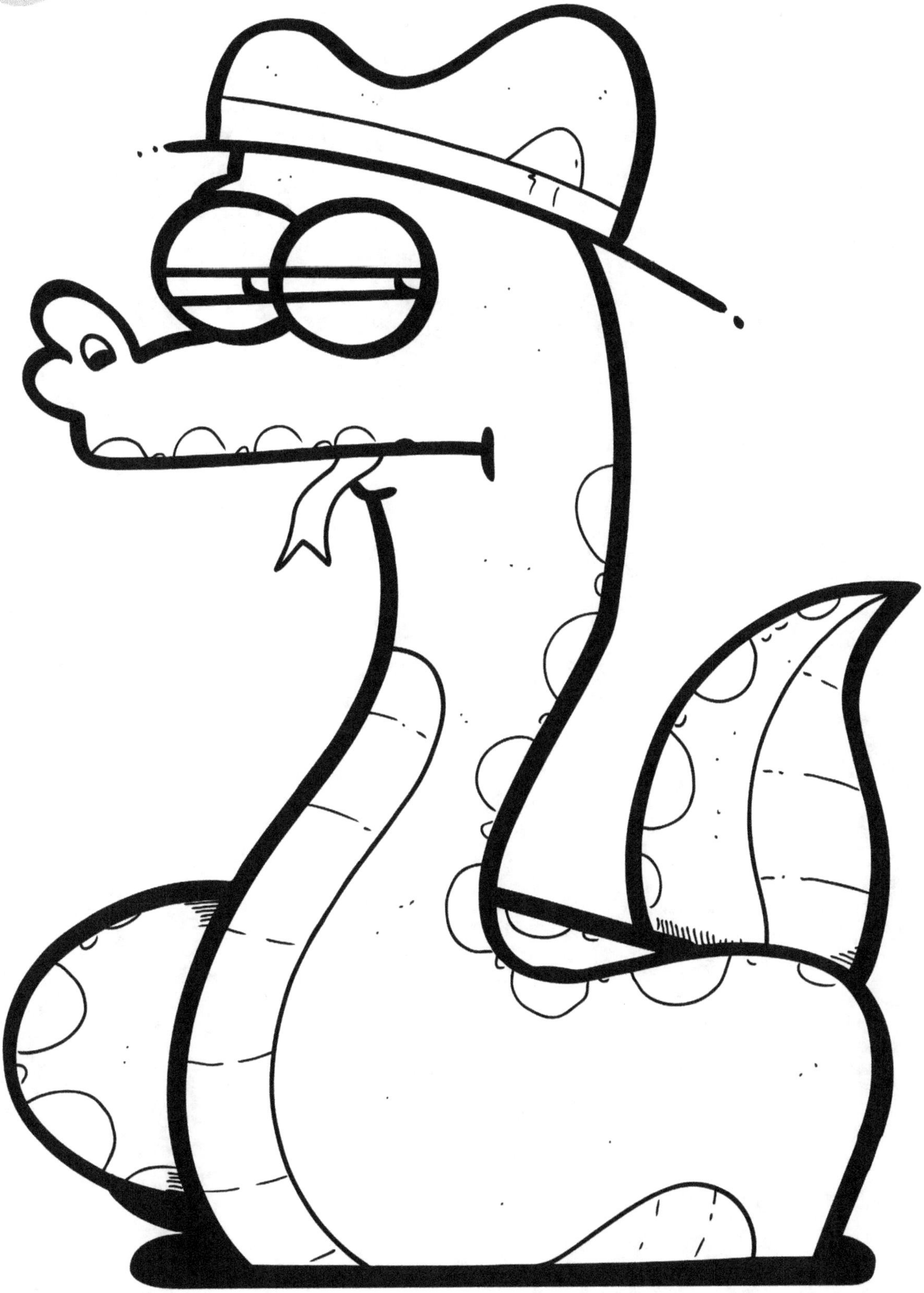

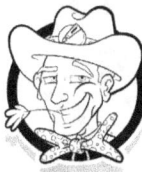 **Does that mean they eat with their nose?** Ha-Ha

? Did you know the **Blue Whale** is the largest animal to have ever lived on Earth? Even bigger than any of the dinosaurs!

So much for getting a **pet** Blue Whale for Christmas.

Did you know **Black Widows** are identified by the red hourglass shape on their back?

Remember, this is your coloring book! You can make the hourglass any color you want!

Did you know most **Parrot** species rely solely on seeds as their main food source?

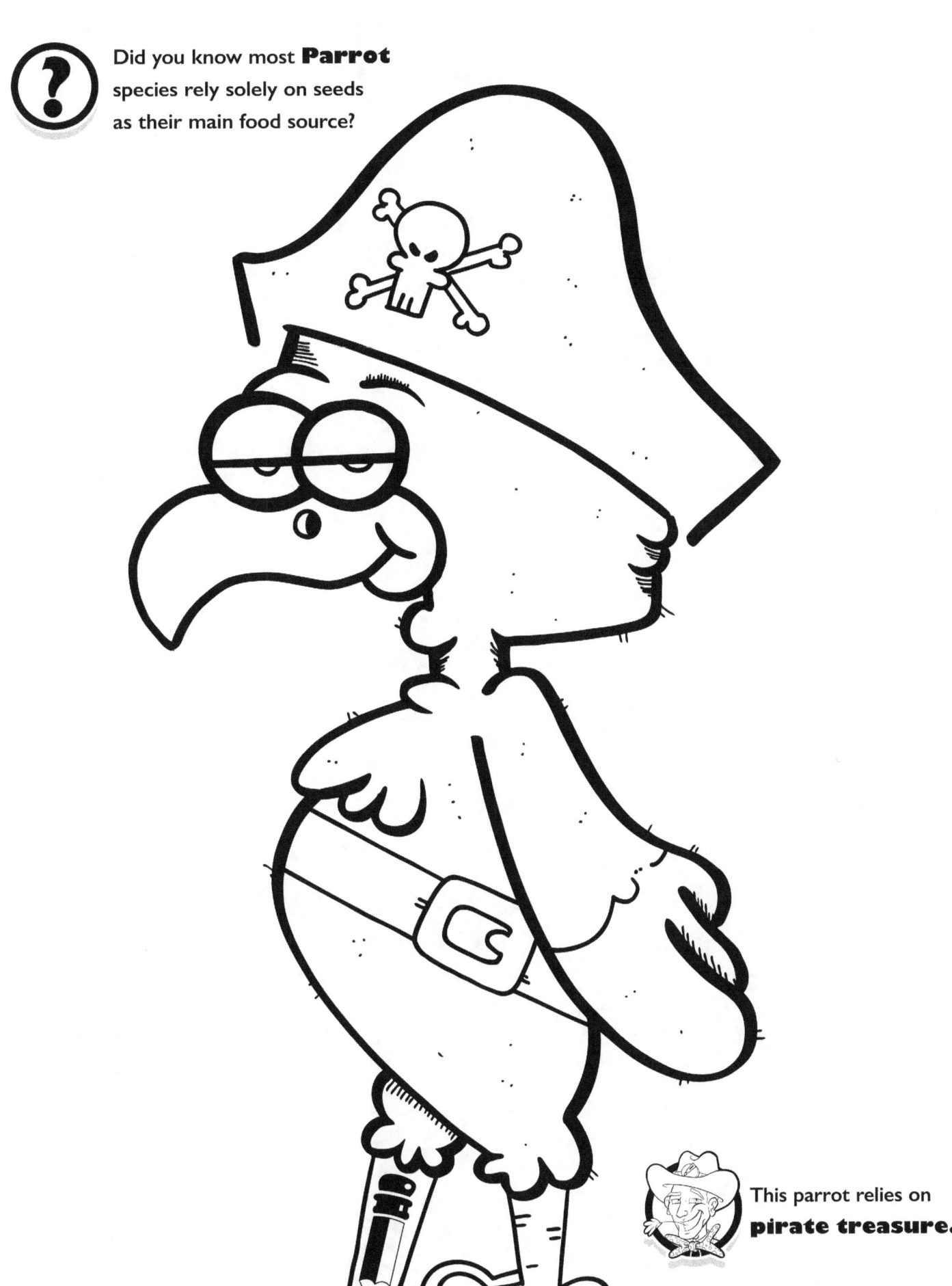

This parrot relies on **pirate treasure.**

 Did you know a male **Rabbit** is called a 'buck,' a female rabbit is called a 'doe' and a baby rabbit is called a 'kit?'

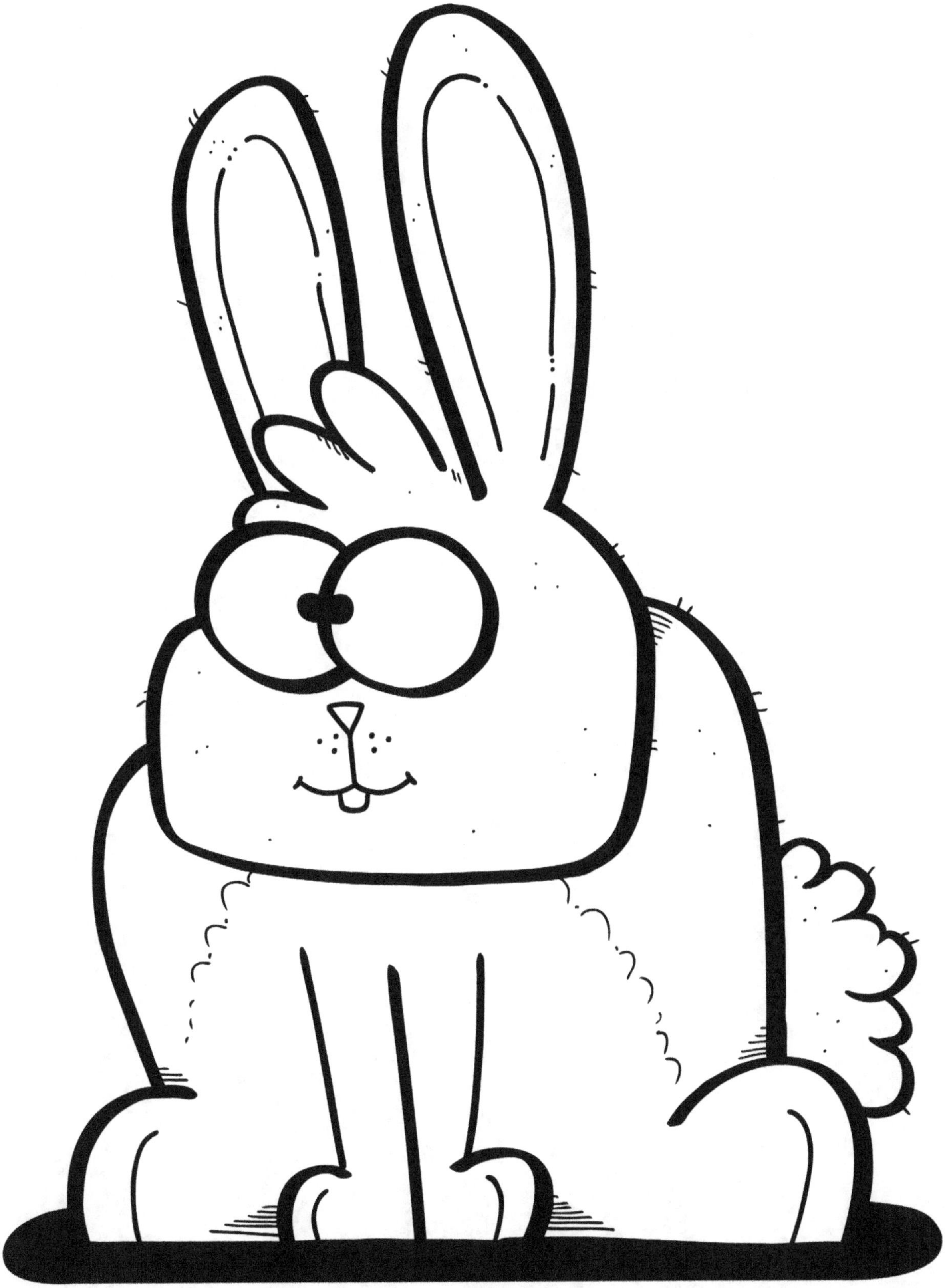

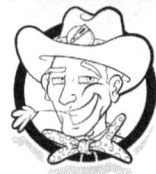 Did you also know **Bugs Bunny** is my favorite bunny of all time?

? Did you know a **Brown Bat** can eat over 1,000 insects every hour?

And I thought I **ate** a lot!

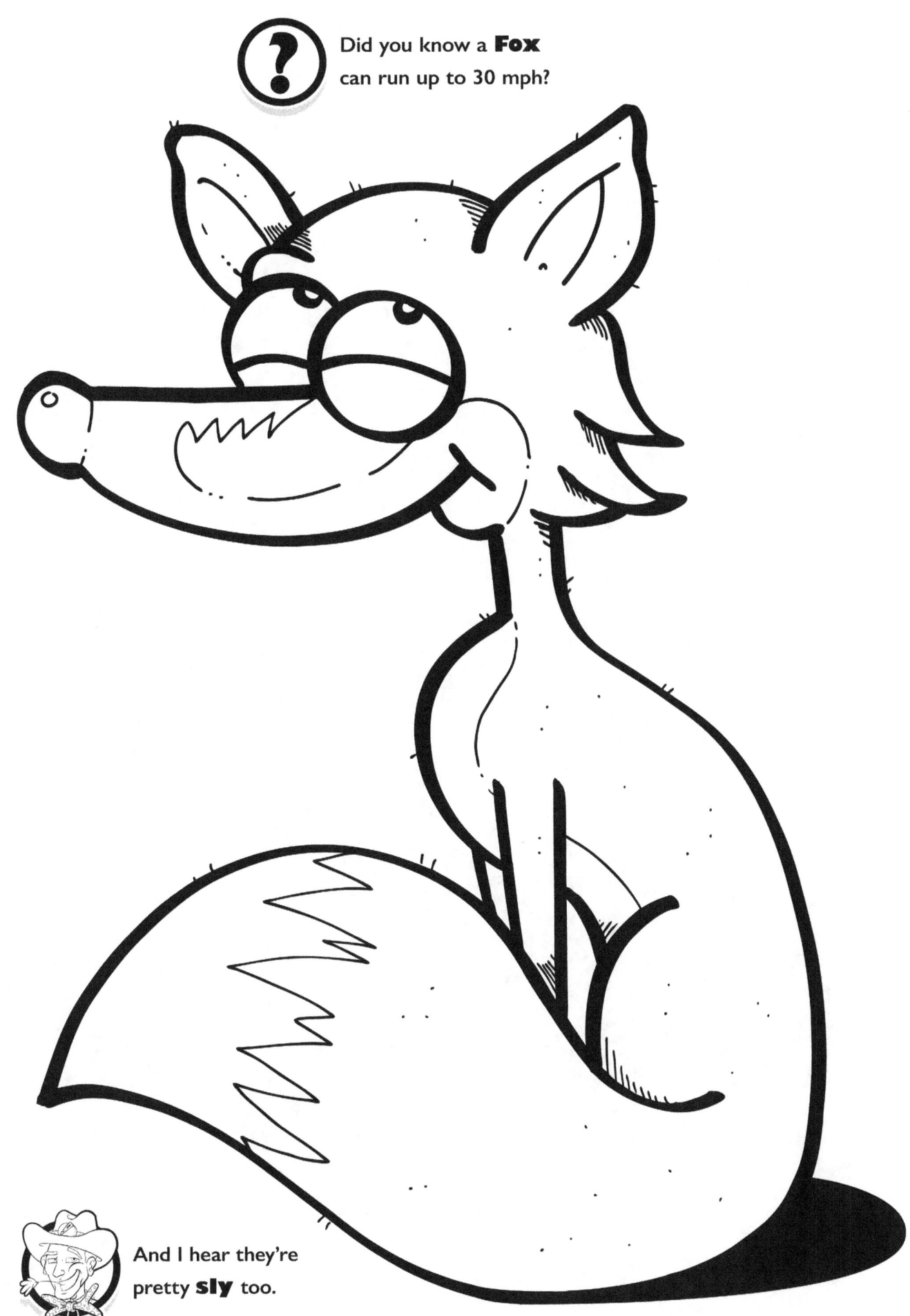

Did you know a **Fox** can run up to 30 mph?

And I hear they're pretty **sly** too.

Did you know a group of Monkeys are known as 'troop?'

This monkey here...
this monkey is **Jim.**

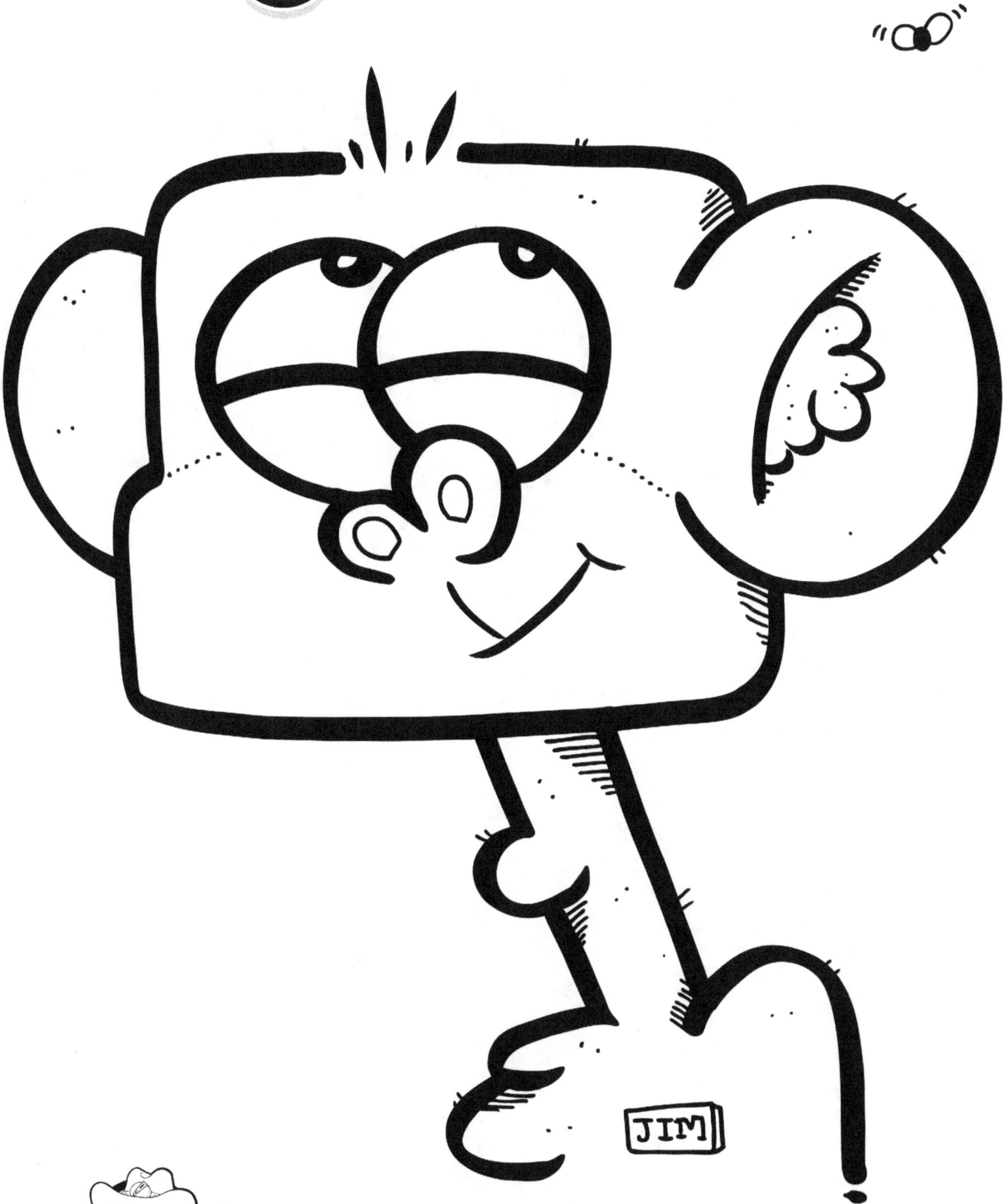

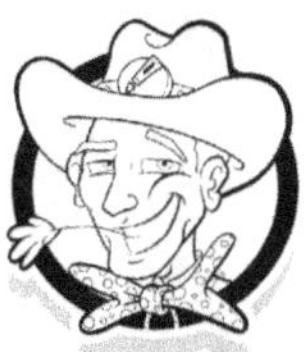

JIM

Did you know **Alligators** have between 74-84 teeth? And they can grow more than 2,000 throughout their lifetime.

He must have the **Tooth Fairy** on speed dial.

Did you know **Pelicans** have the largest bill of any bird?

I wonder how many **cookies** you could fit in his mouth?

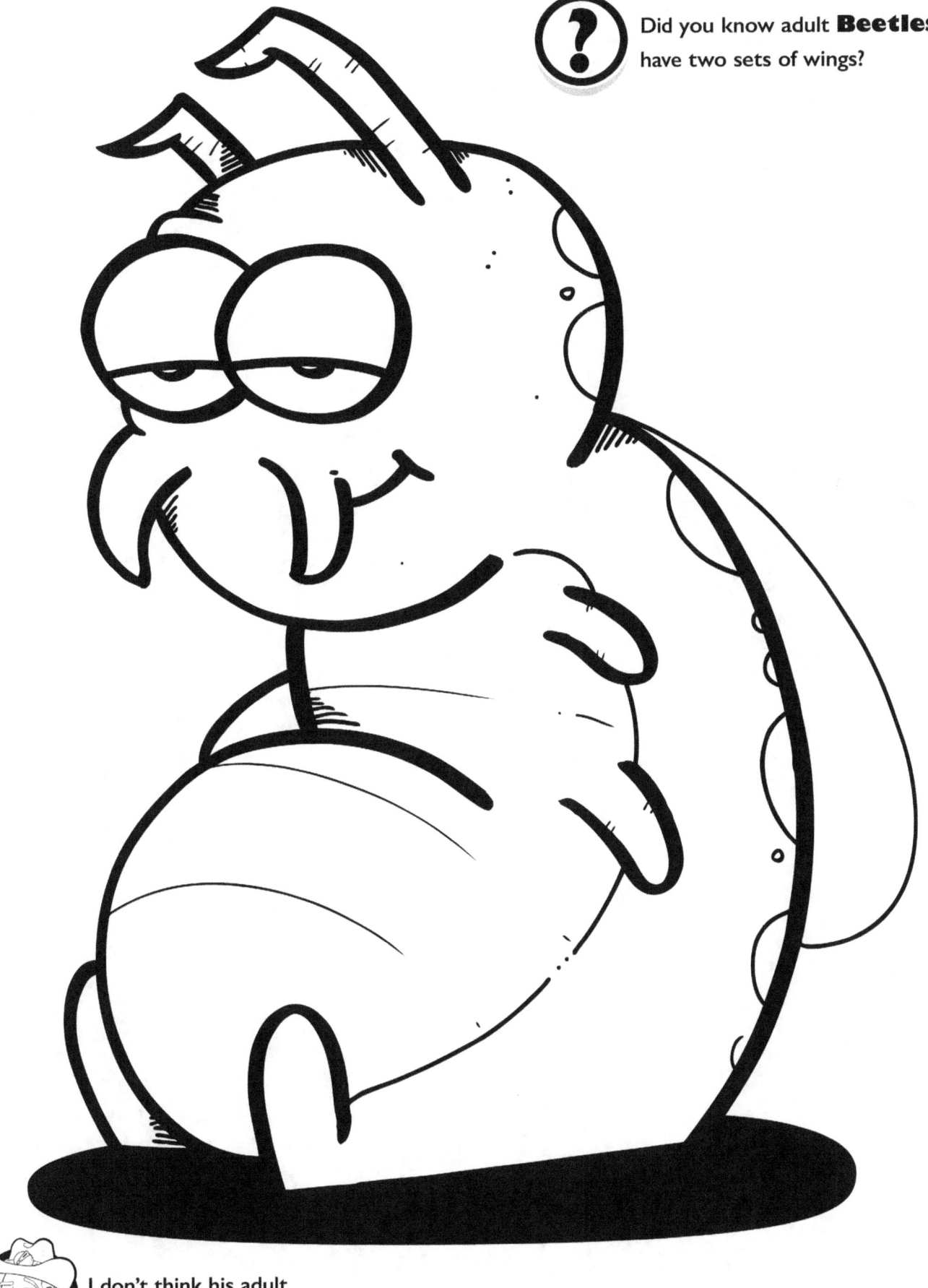

? Did you know adult **Beetles** have two sets of wings?

I don't think his adult **wings** work.

Did you know **Turtles** have been around for over 200 million years?

Whoa! That is a lot of birthday parties!

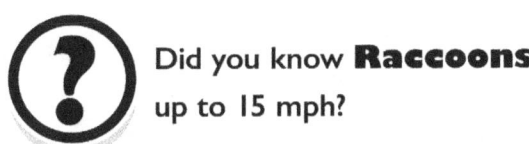

Did you know **Raccoons** can run up to 15 mph?

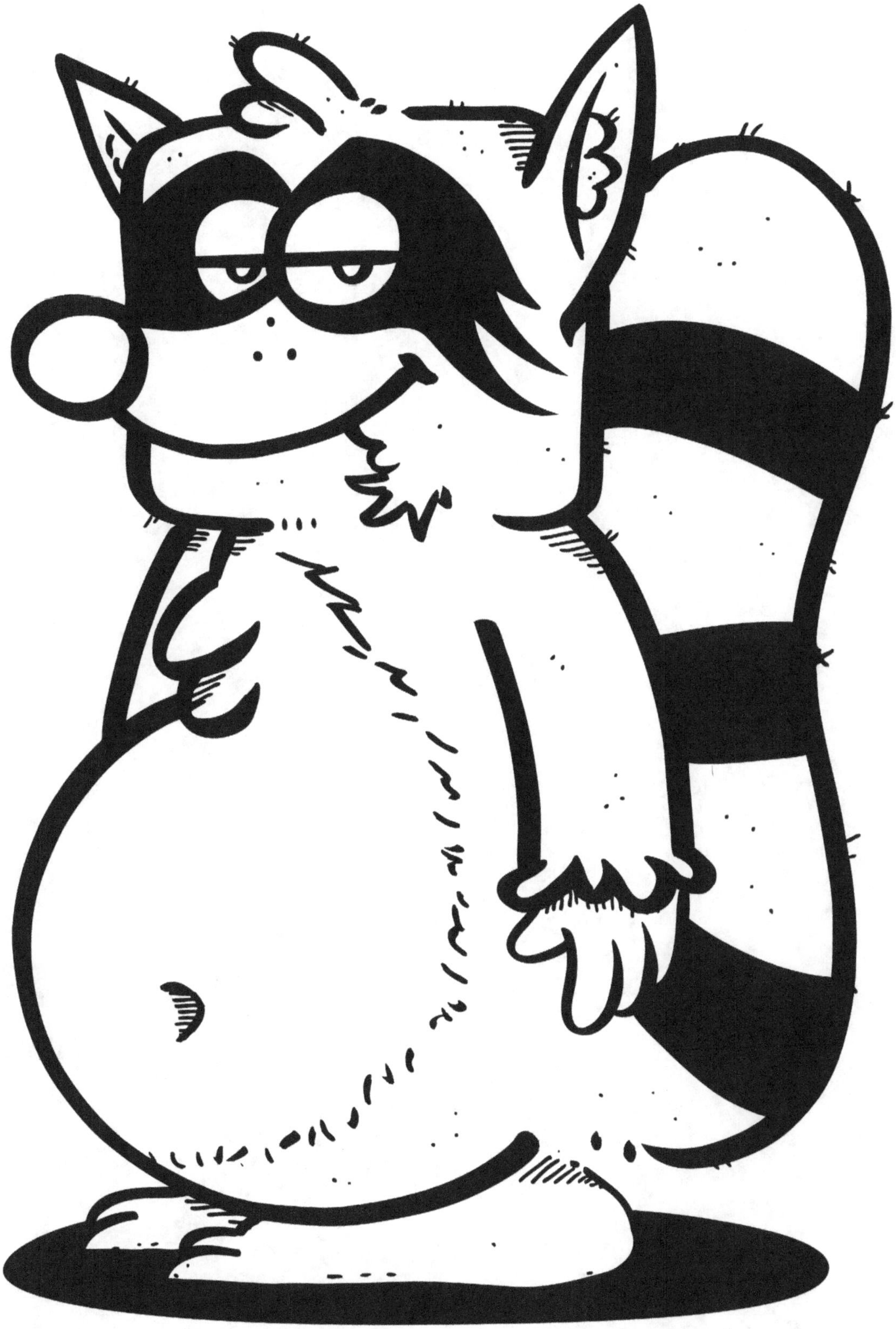

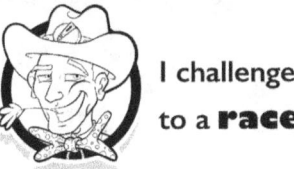

I challenge any raccoon to a **race!**

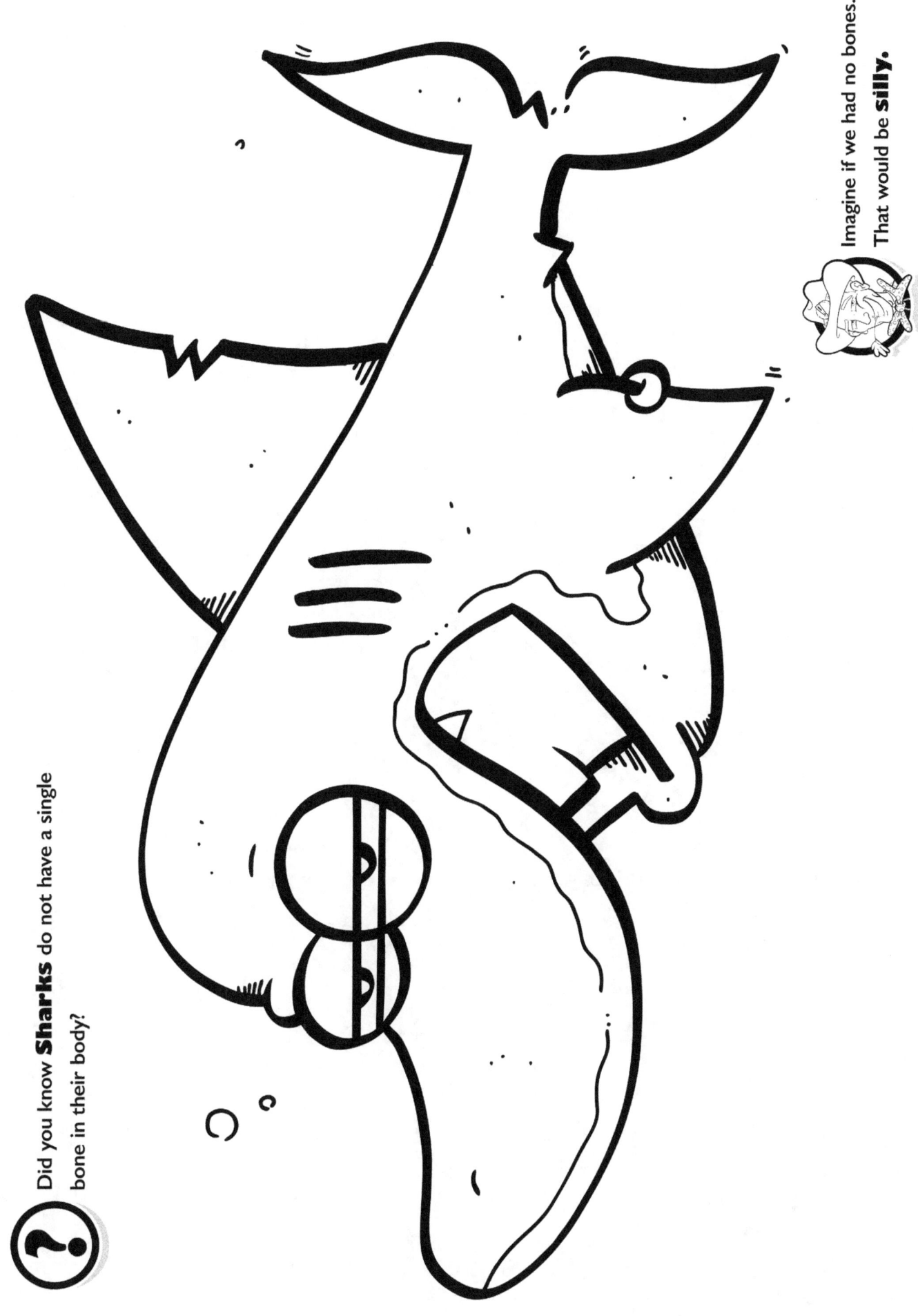

Did you know **Sharks** do not have a single bone in their body?

Imagine if we had no bones. That would be **silly.**

? Did you know the **Dodo Bird** lived in complete isolation all because they couldn't fly to their neighboring islands?

Aww, poor dodo bird.

Did you know that **Polar Bears** have black skin? Yup, and thier fur is actually transparent even though it appears white.

Baby polar bears are the best when they **tumble** down hills!

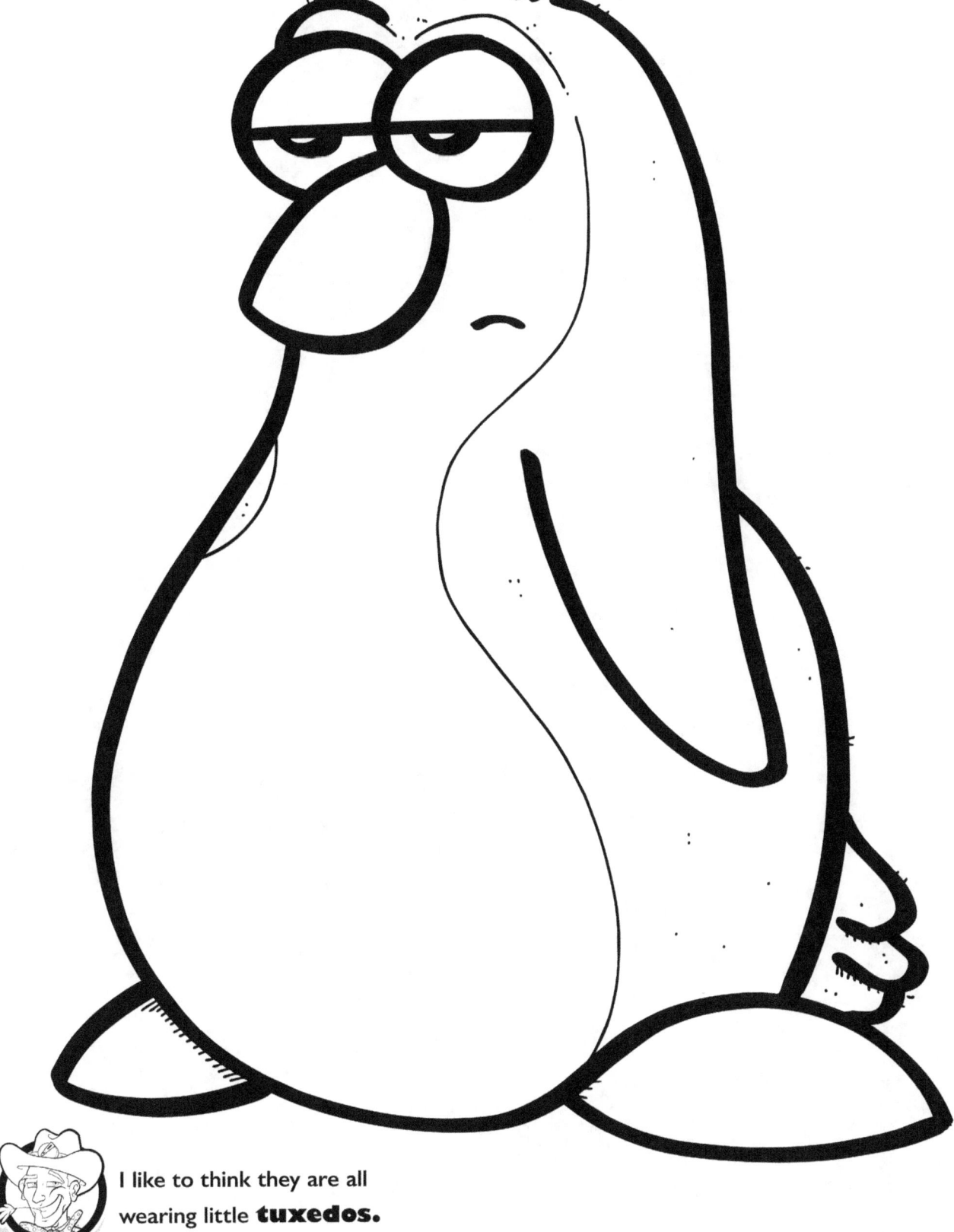

Did you know that male **Penguins** will incubate the eggs while the female penguins hunt?

I like to think they are all wearing little **tuxedos.**

Did you know **Chickens** have an excellent memory? They can recognize more than 100 different faces!

No wonder they always say **hi** to me!

? Did you know this fictional animal is referred to as a **Meowmaid?** Well, Mrs. Meowmaid to be exact.

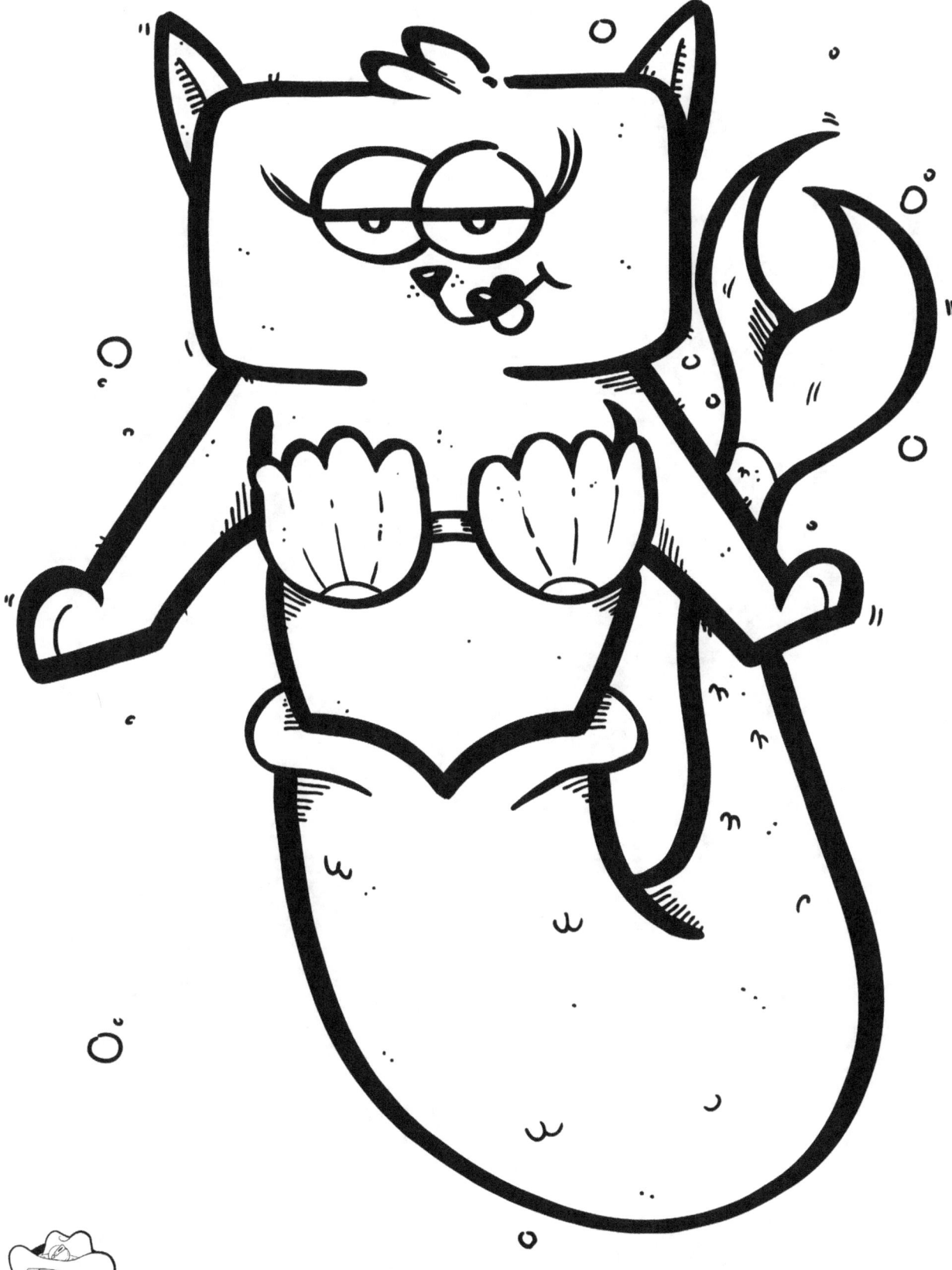

Isn't she **funny?** She is half cat, half mermaid.

Did you know **Bulldogs** are poor swimmers? This is mainly due to their short legs and heavy bodies.

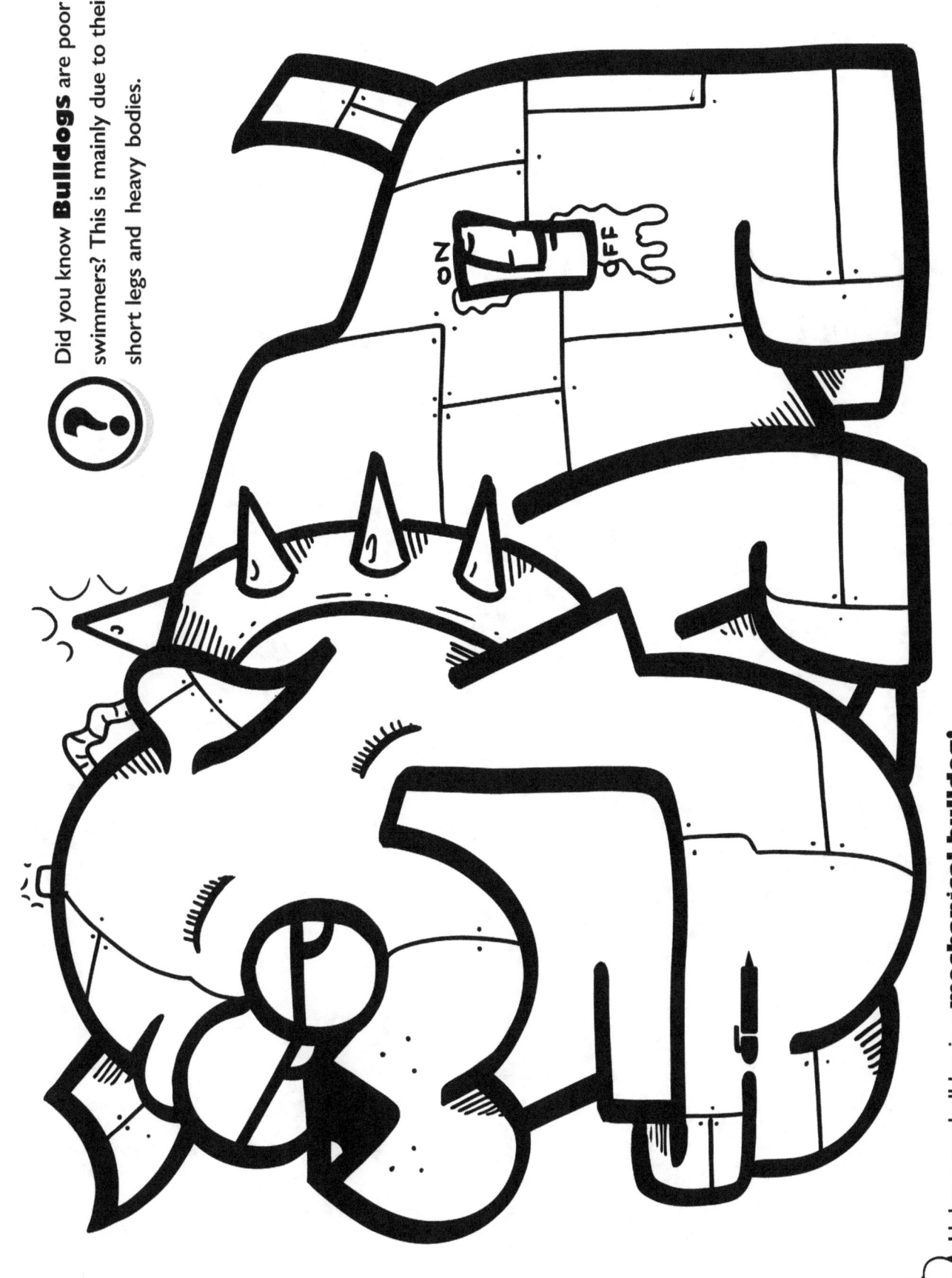

Unless your bulldog is a **mechanical bulldog!**

Wait, maybe don't put your robot dog in water.

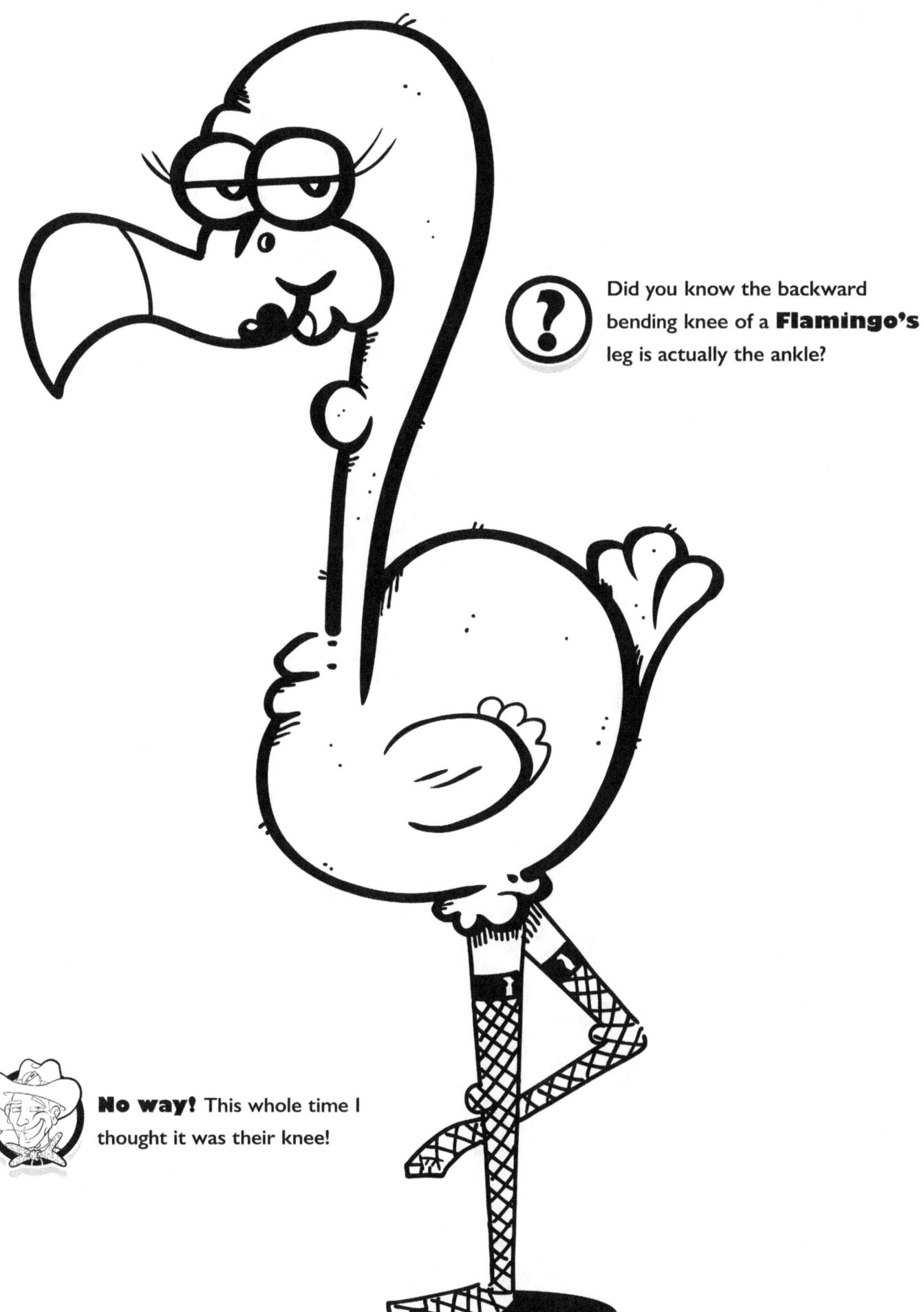

Did you know the backward bending knee of a **Flamingo's** leg is actually the ankle?

No way! This whole time I thought it was their knee!

Did you know this is **Mr. Meowmaid?**

What gave it away? Is it because he is also half cat, half **mermaid?**

Did you know the **Ostrich** is the world's largest bird? Yup! And even though they can't fly, they can run over 40 mph!

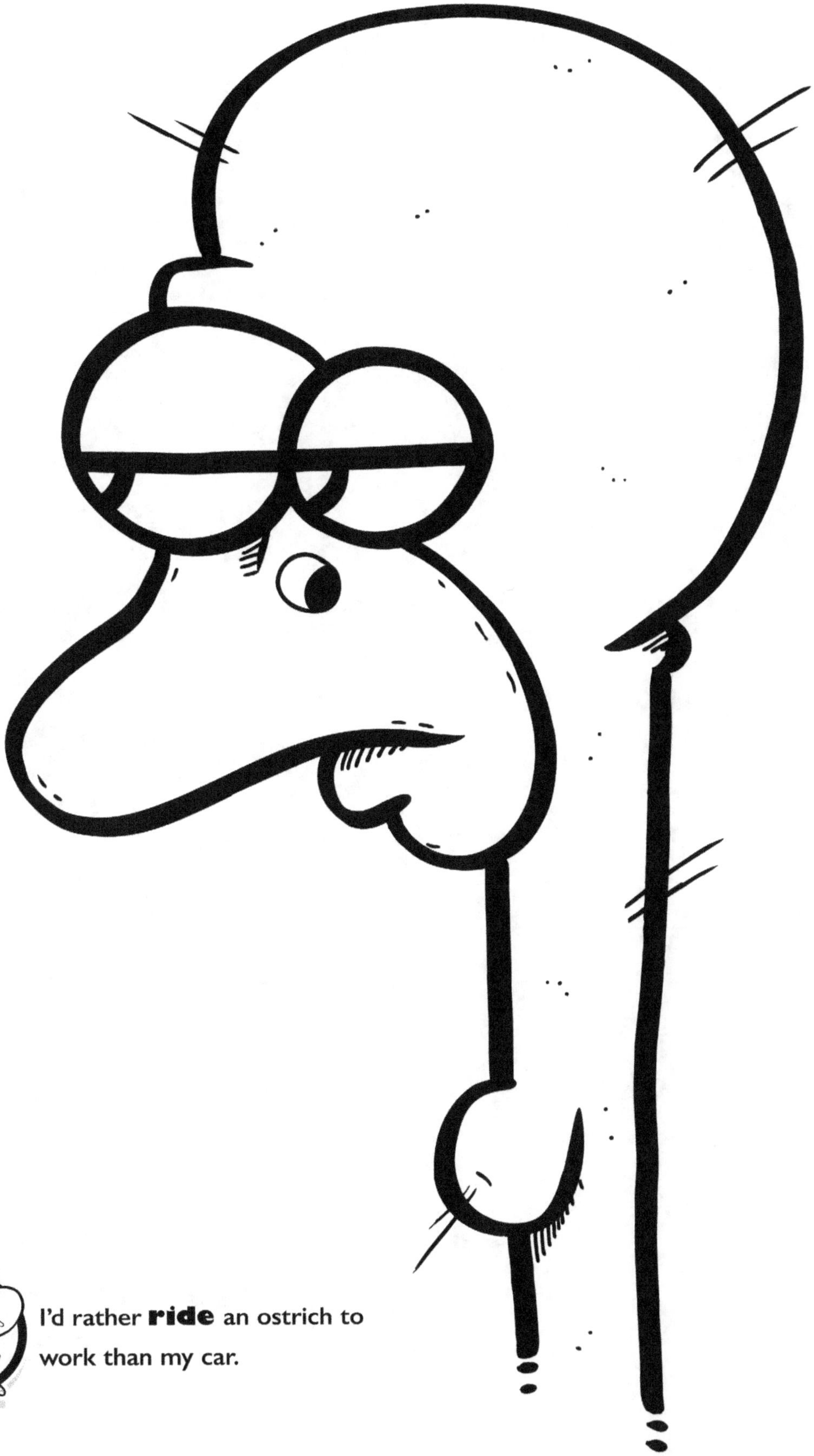

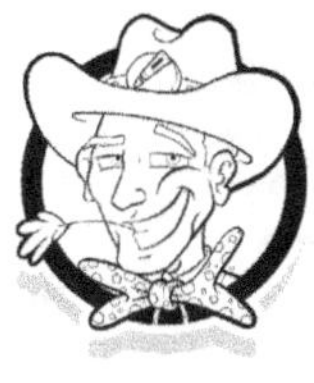

I'd rather **ride** an ostrich to work than my car.

Did you know **Chili Chinchilla** was a cartoon character created by Mr. Gray when he was in Art School!

Now it's your turn! What silly characters can you **create?**

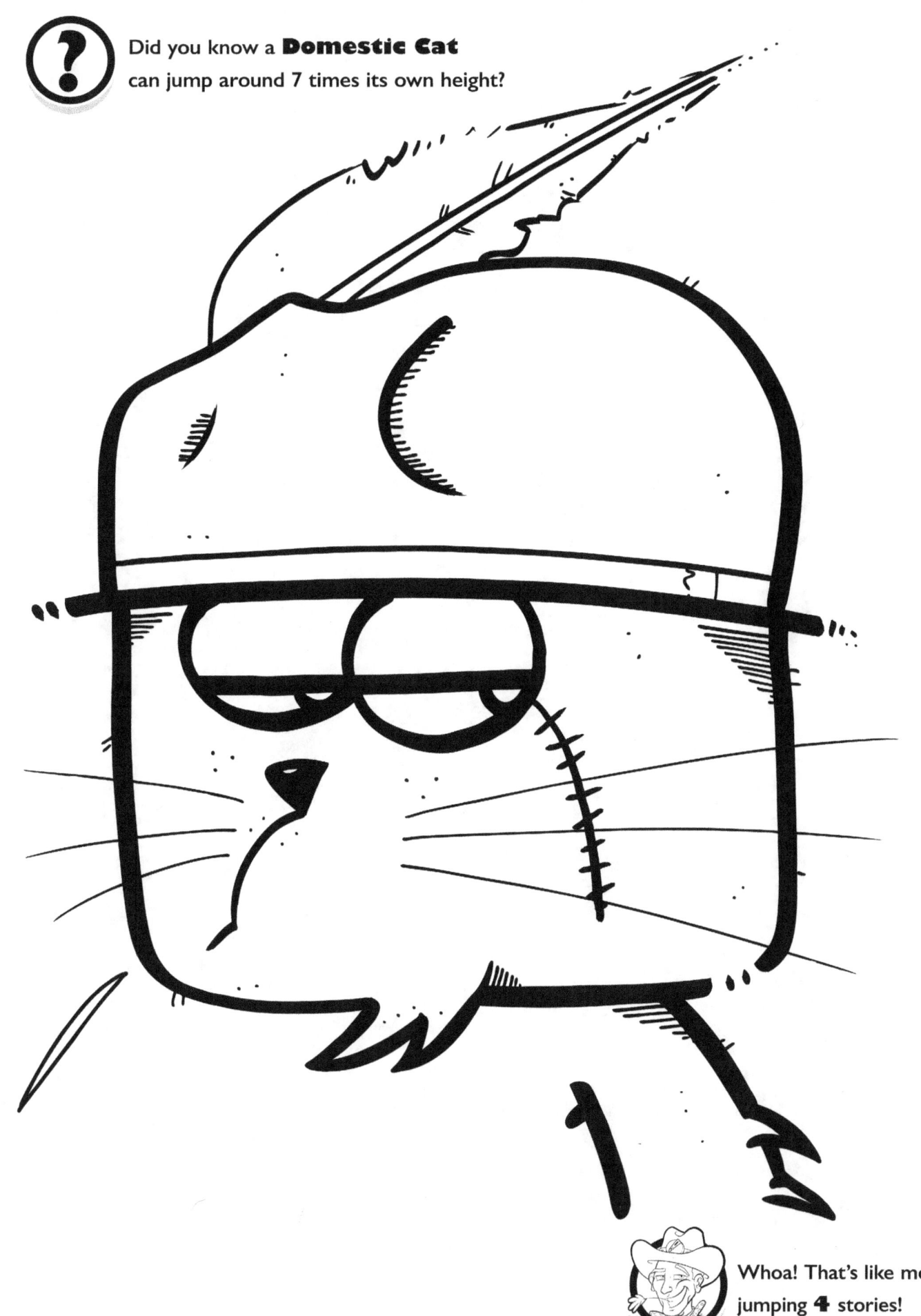

Whoa! That's like me jumping **4** stories!

① Did you know a male **Horse** is called a 'Stallion' and a female horse is called a 'Mare?'

I once rode a horse; I named him **Bubbles.**

? Did you know **Goldfish** have teeth in their throat that are used to help crush their food?

I think this goldfish uses his special **dentures** to crush his food.

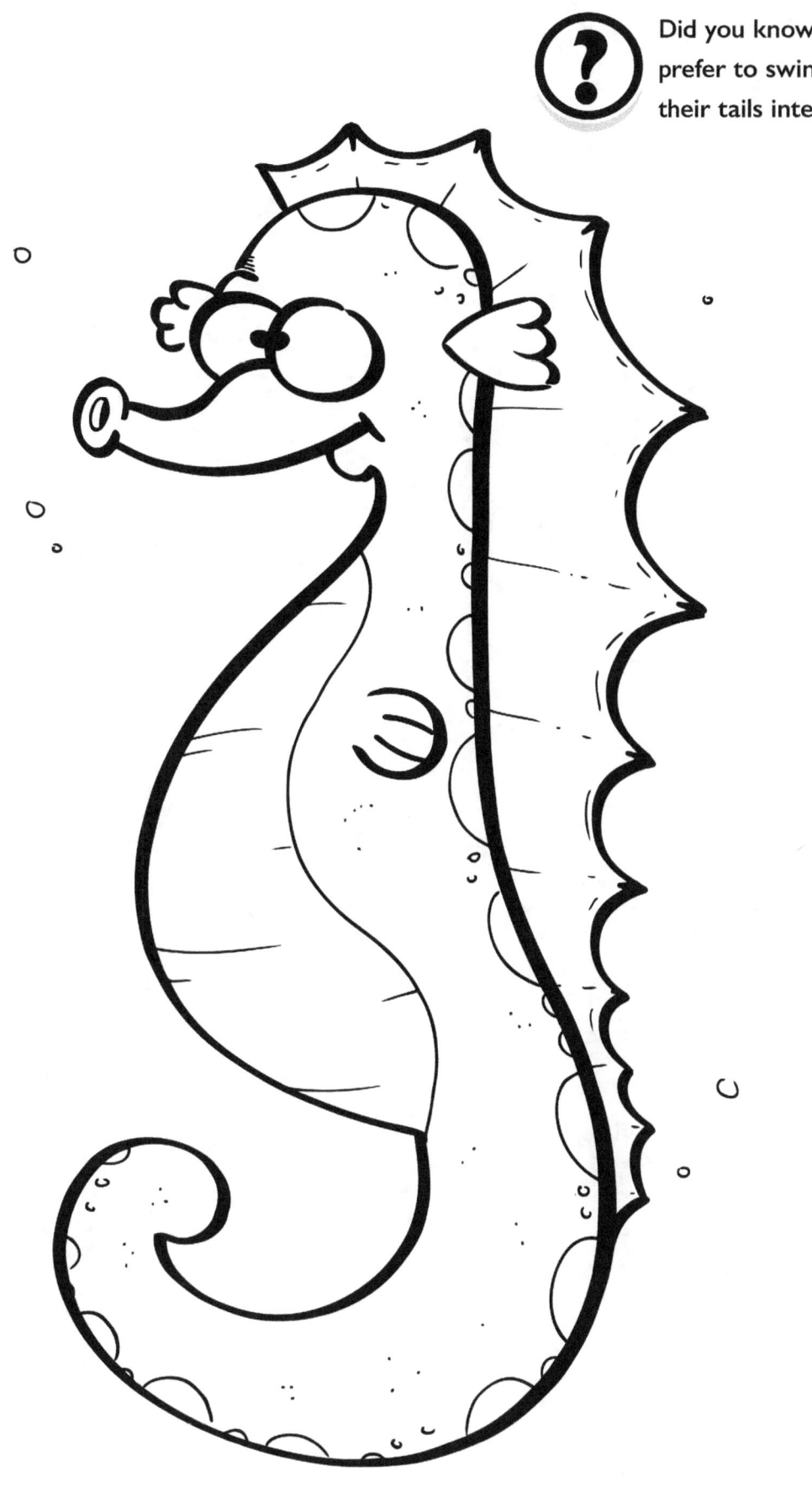

? Did you know **Seahorses** prefer to swim in pairs with their tails interlocked?

Imagine if we walked around with our feet **tied** together!

? Did you know **Sloths** only go the bathroom once a week?

They must save a fortune on **toilet paper.**

? Did you know there are over 1 billion **Sheep** in the world?

Imagine trying to count everyone beford bed!

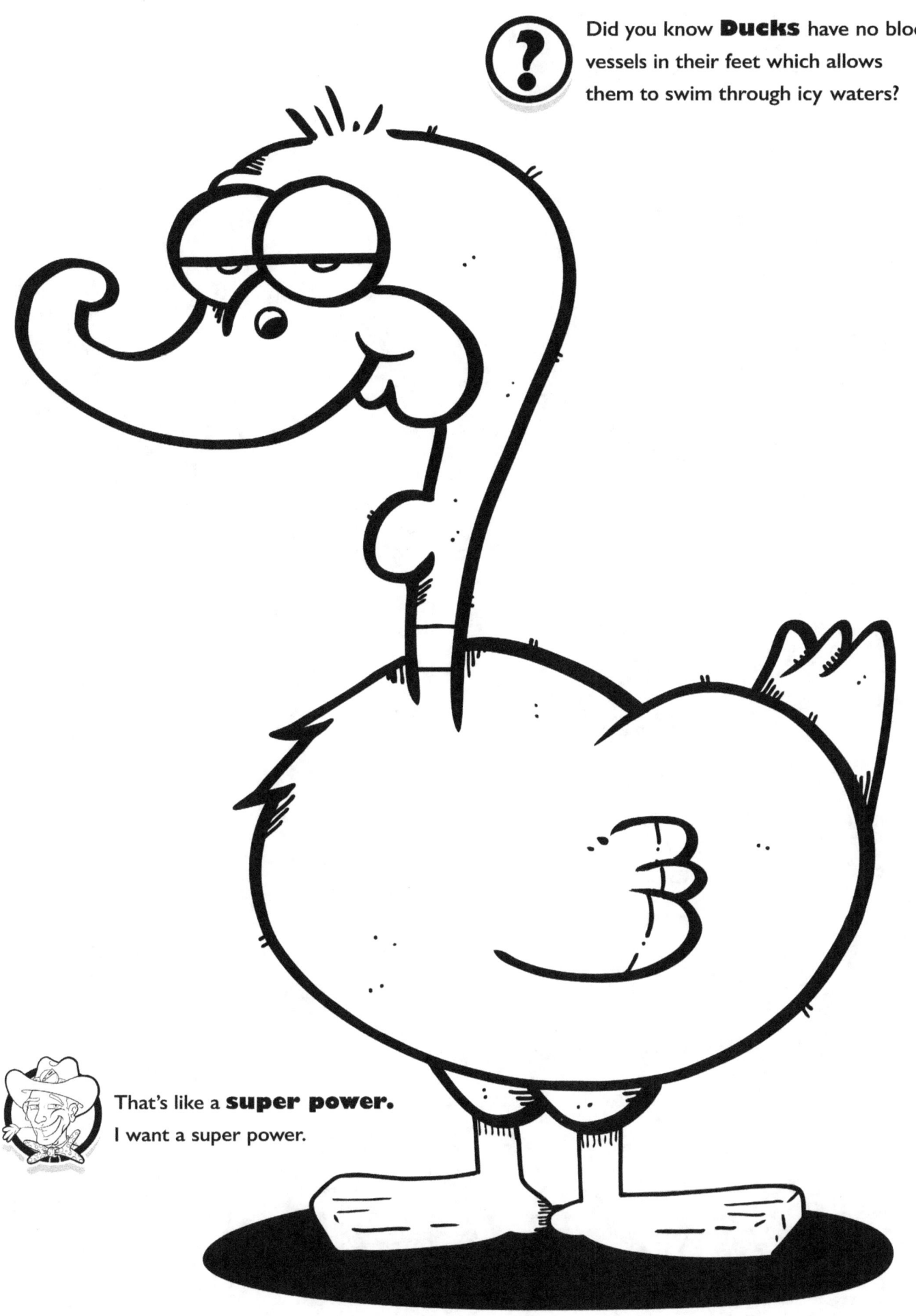

Did you know **Ducks** have no blood vessels in their feet which allows them to swim through icy waters?

That's like a **super power.**
I want a super power.

? Did you know the lifespan of a **Housefly** is generally between 15-30 days?

I hope this fly makes it to
Cinco de Mayo.

Did you know **Crows** are considered song-birds?

I'd pay to see that **concert.**

? Did you know 'Dog-tired' is an old English phrase meaning to be physically exhausted?

Awe...sleepy pup.

 Did you know in places like Great Britain and Ireland, **Black Cats** are considered good luck?

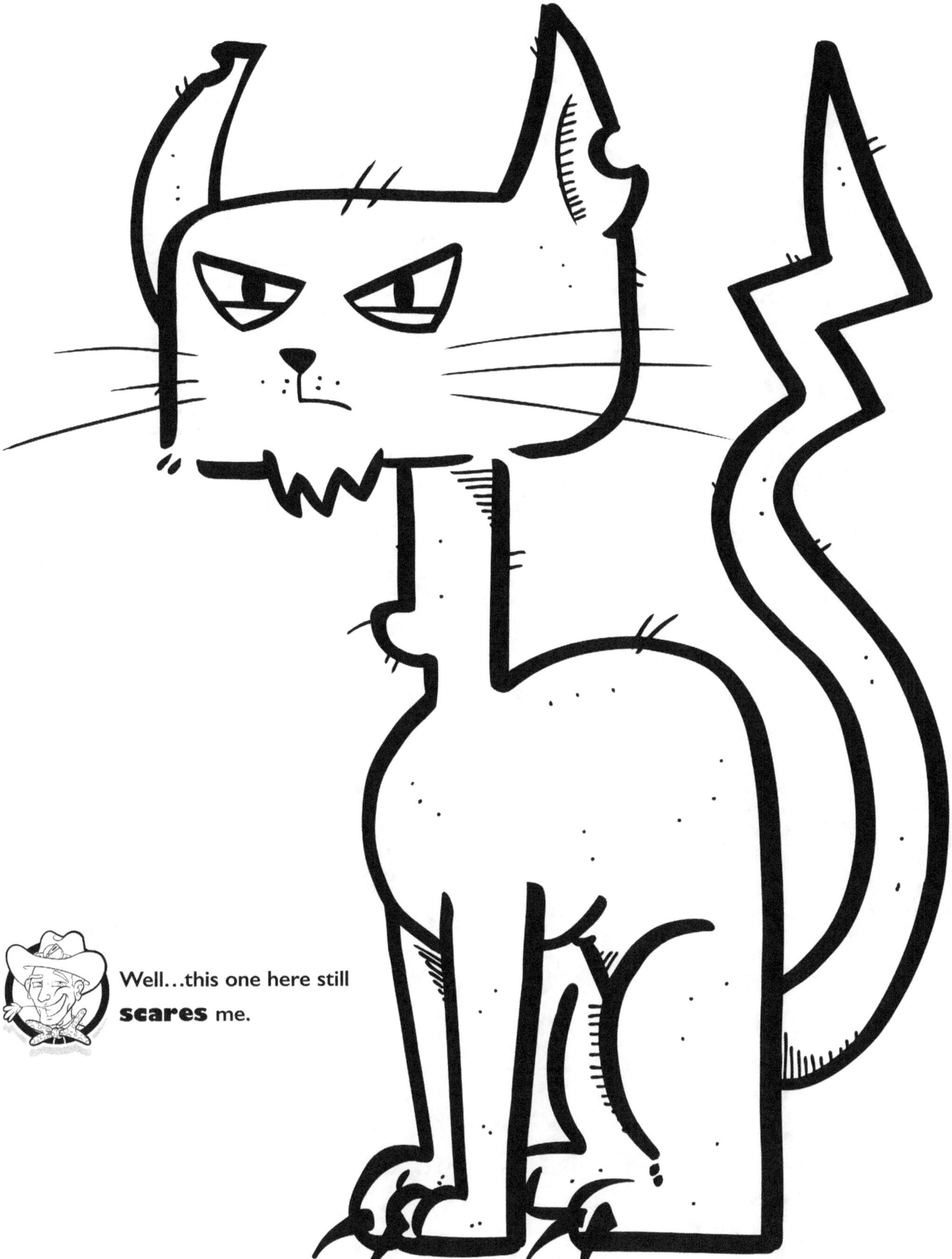

Well…this one here still **scares** me.

 Did you know a **Toucan's** bill is made of keratin, the same material as our finger nails?

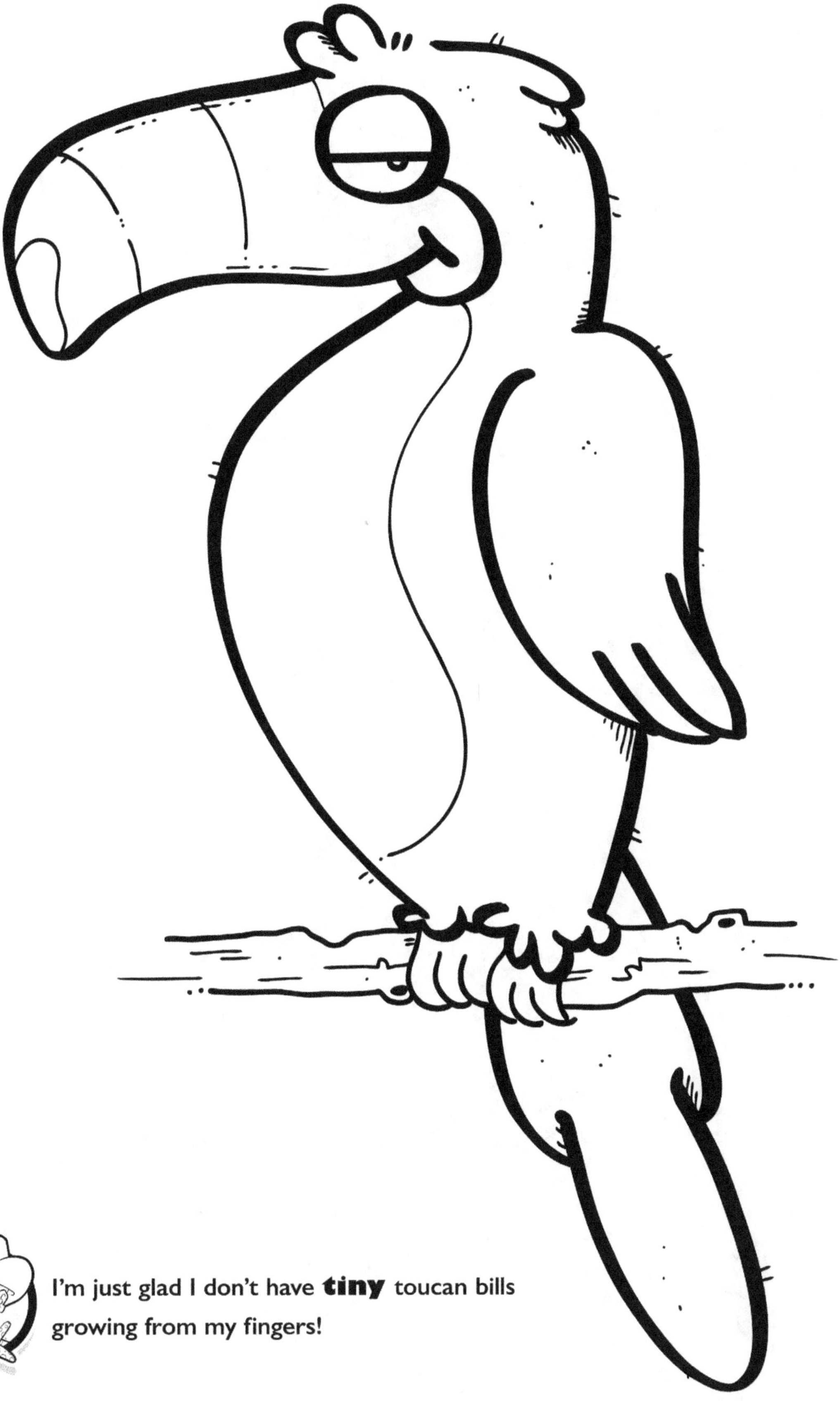

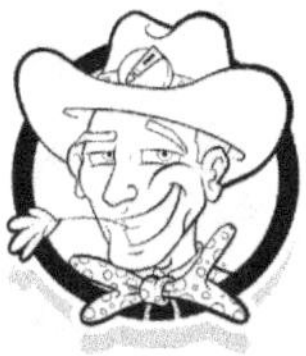

I'm just glad I don't have **tiny** toucan bills growing from my fingers!

Did you know that only males are 'Peacocks?' Females are 'peahens' and babies are 'peachicks.'

I wish I had colorful peacock feathers.

? Did you know during hibernation **Bears** do not go to the bathroom?

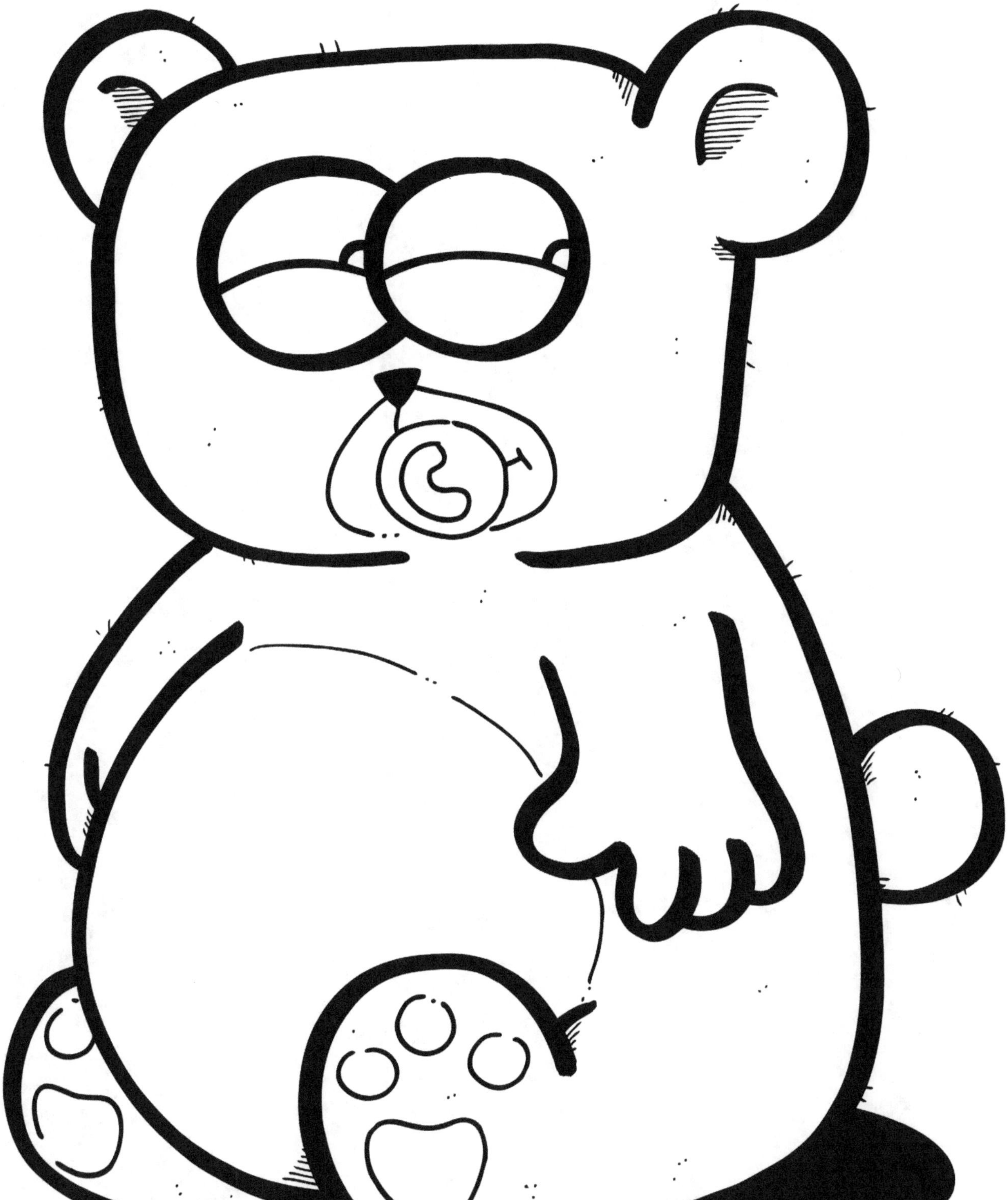

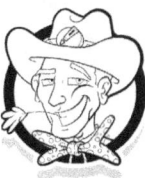 **No way!** I could never hold it for that long!

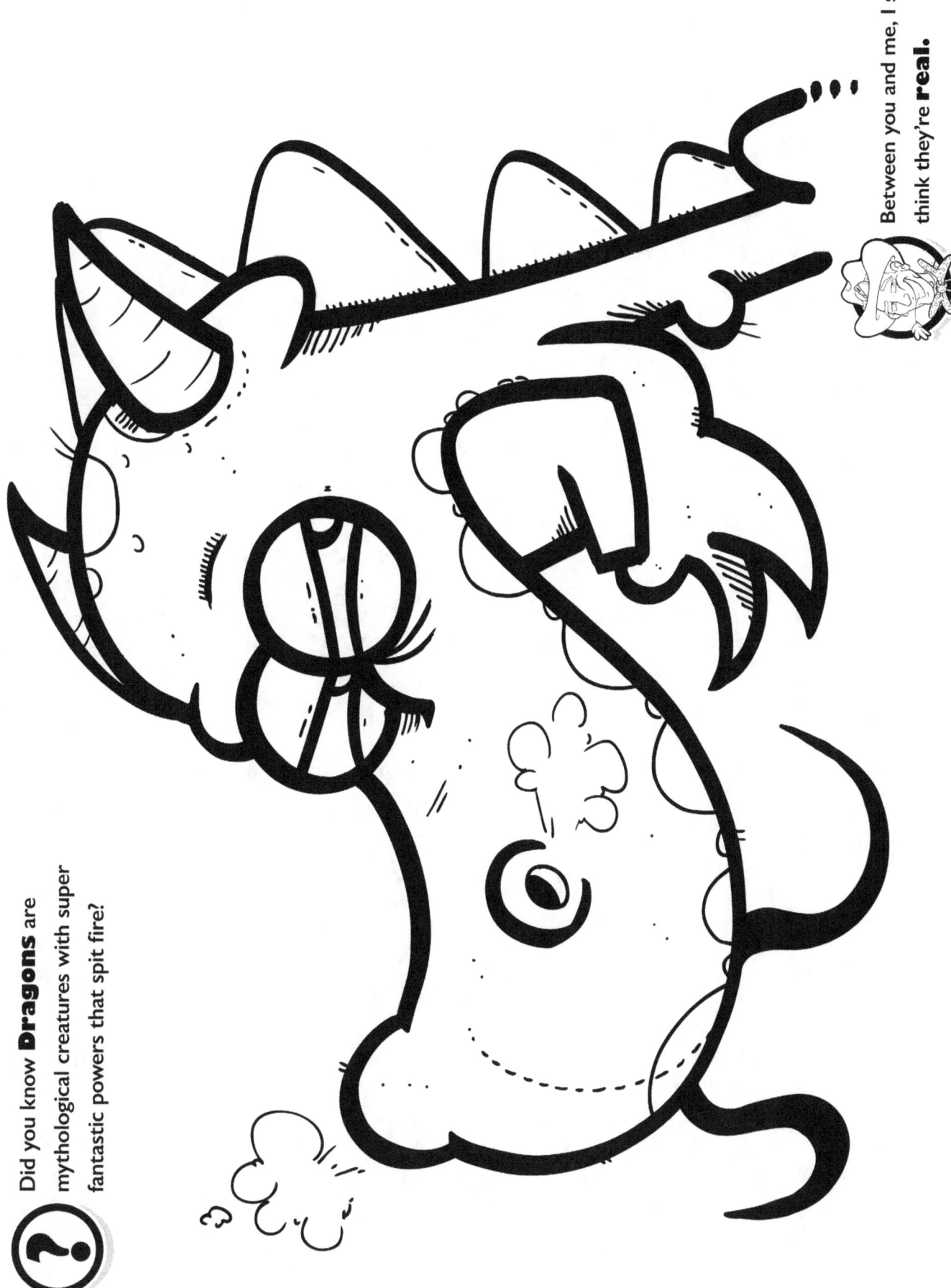

Did you know **Dragons** are mythological creatures with super fantastic powers that spit fire?

Between you and me, I still think they're **real.**

 Do you know how to distinguish between a monkey and an **Ape?** Monkeys have tails and apes do not.

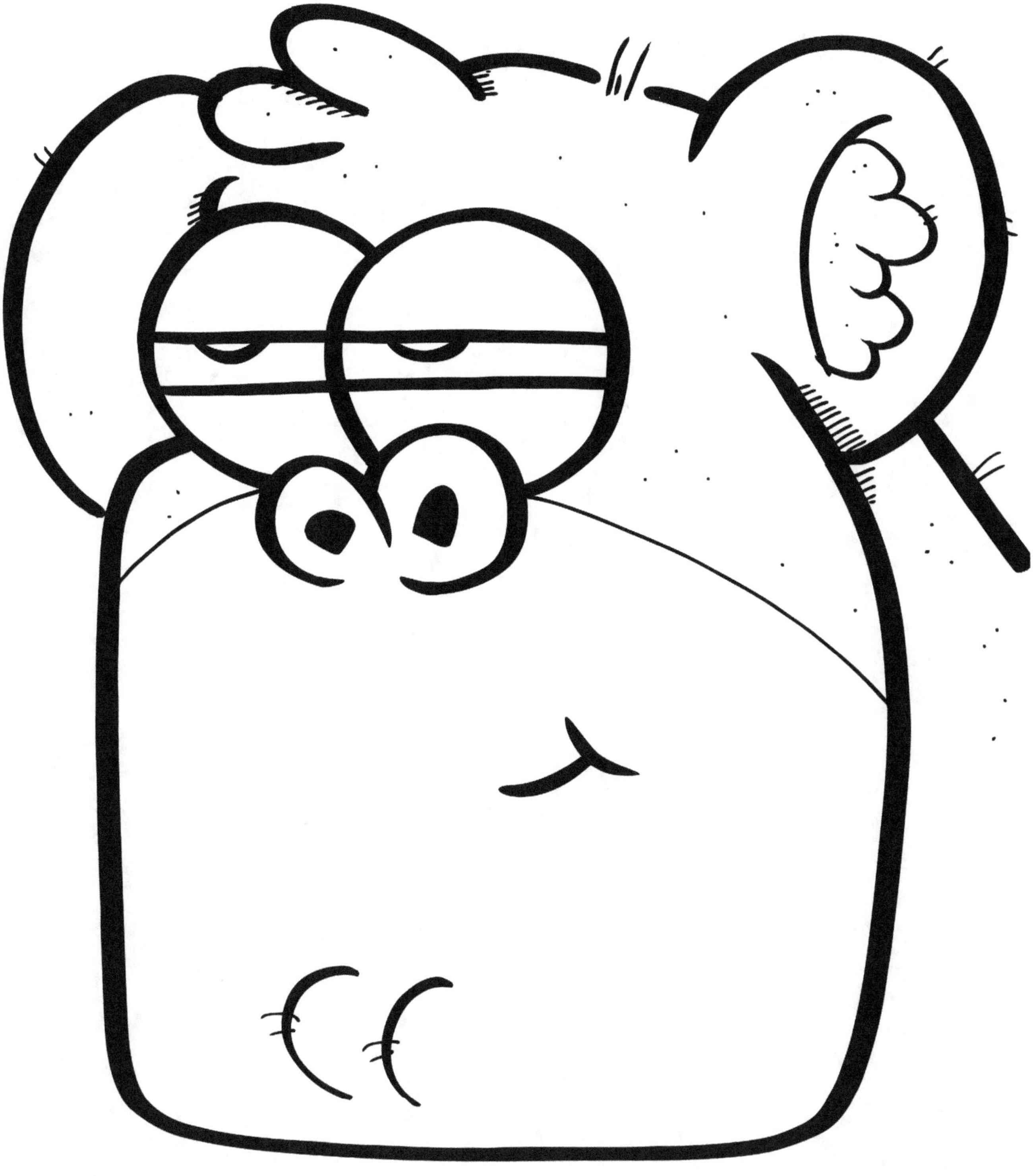

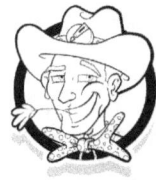 I wish I had a tail to **swing** from tree to tree.

Did you know a **wolf** pup's eyes are blue at birth and change to yellow around eight months old?

?

I hear they also like to **huff and puff** and blow houses to the ground too.

? Did you know **Camel** humps do not store water? They store fat that helps keep their body cool in the desert.

And I thought the humps were full of **Skittles.**

? Did you know a **Pig** squeal is 3 decibels higher than the sound of a supersonic airliner?

That is **loud!**

 Did you know a **Rat** tail helps regulate their body temperature and even helps them communicate?

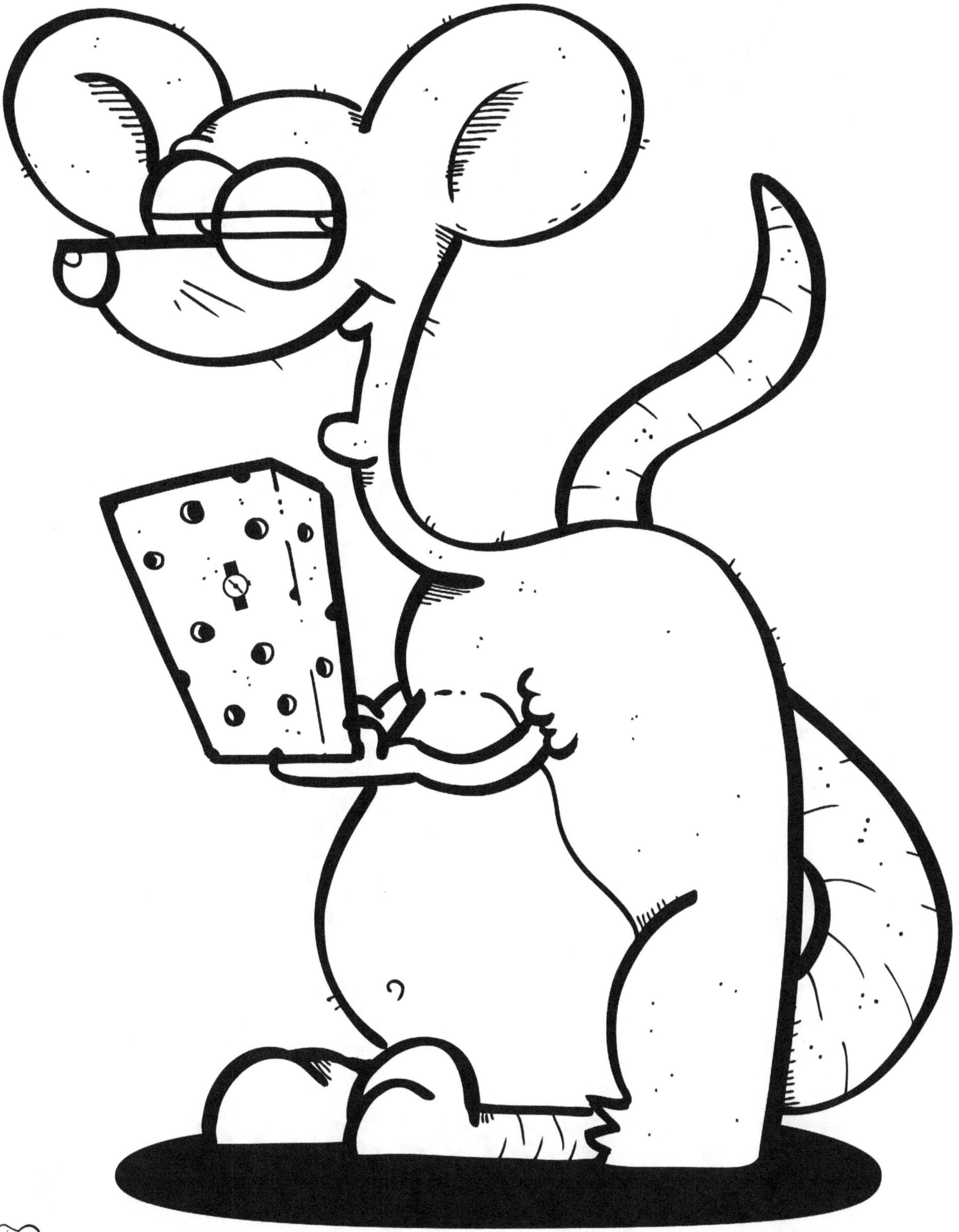

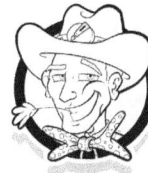 And did you know they also love **cheese?**

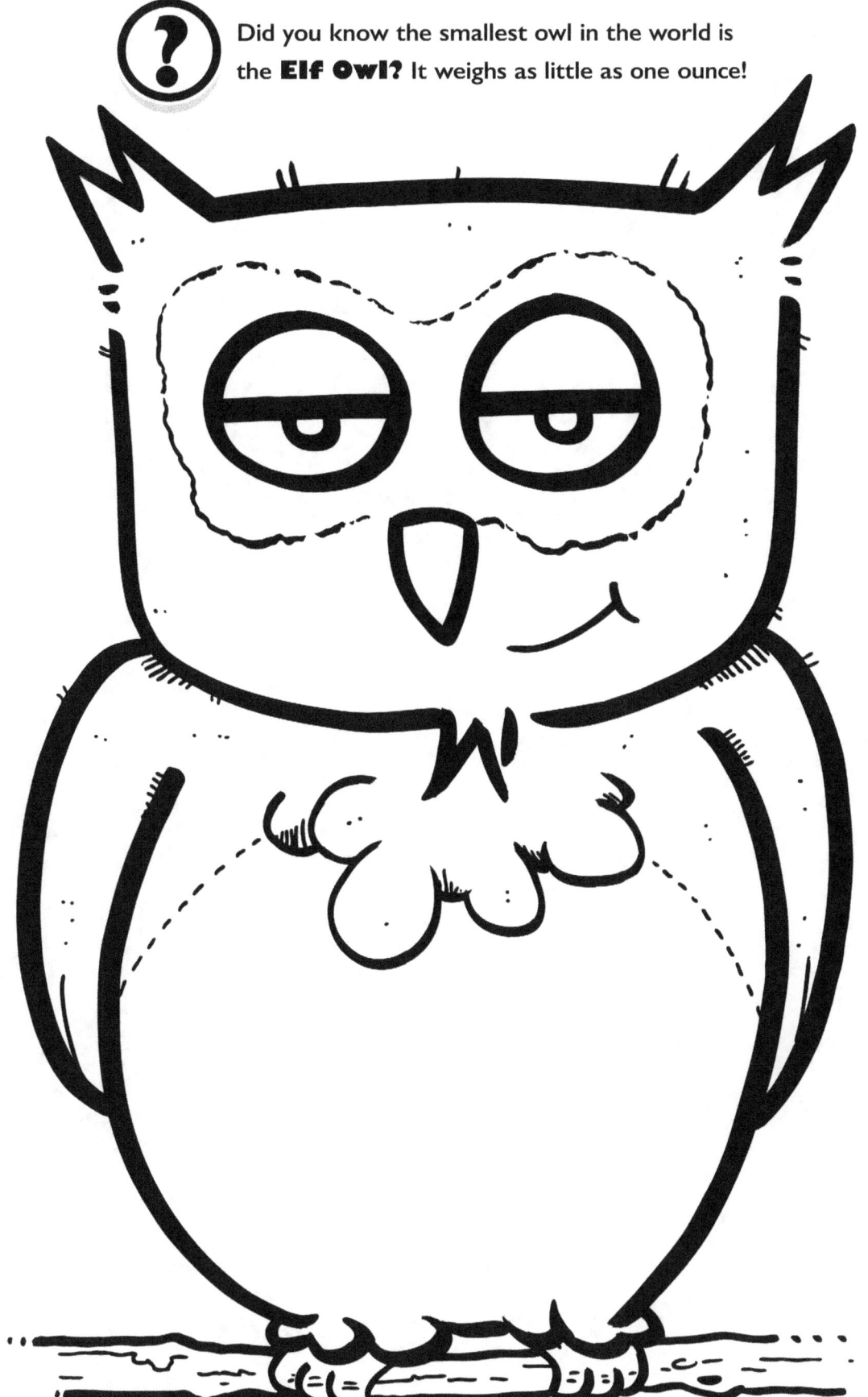

? Did you know the smallest owl in the world is the **Elf Owl?** It weighs as little as one ounce!

He could fit in a **tea cup!**

? Did you know the average **Bull** weighs anywhere from 1,600-1,800 pounds?

Whoa. That's like ten of me combined.

Did you know a group of **Vultures** is called a 'venue' and when they are circling in the air they are called a 'kettle?'

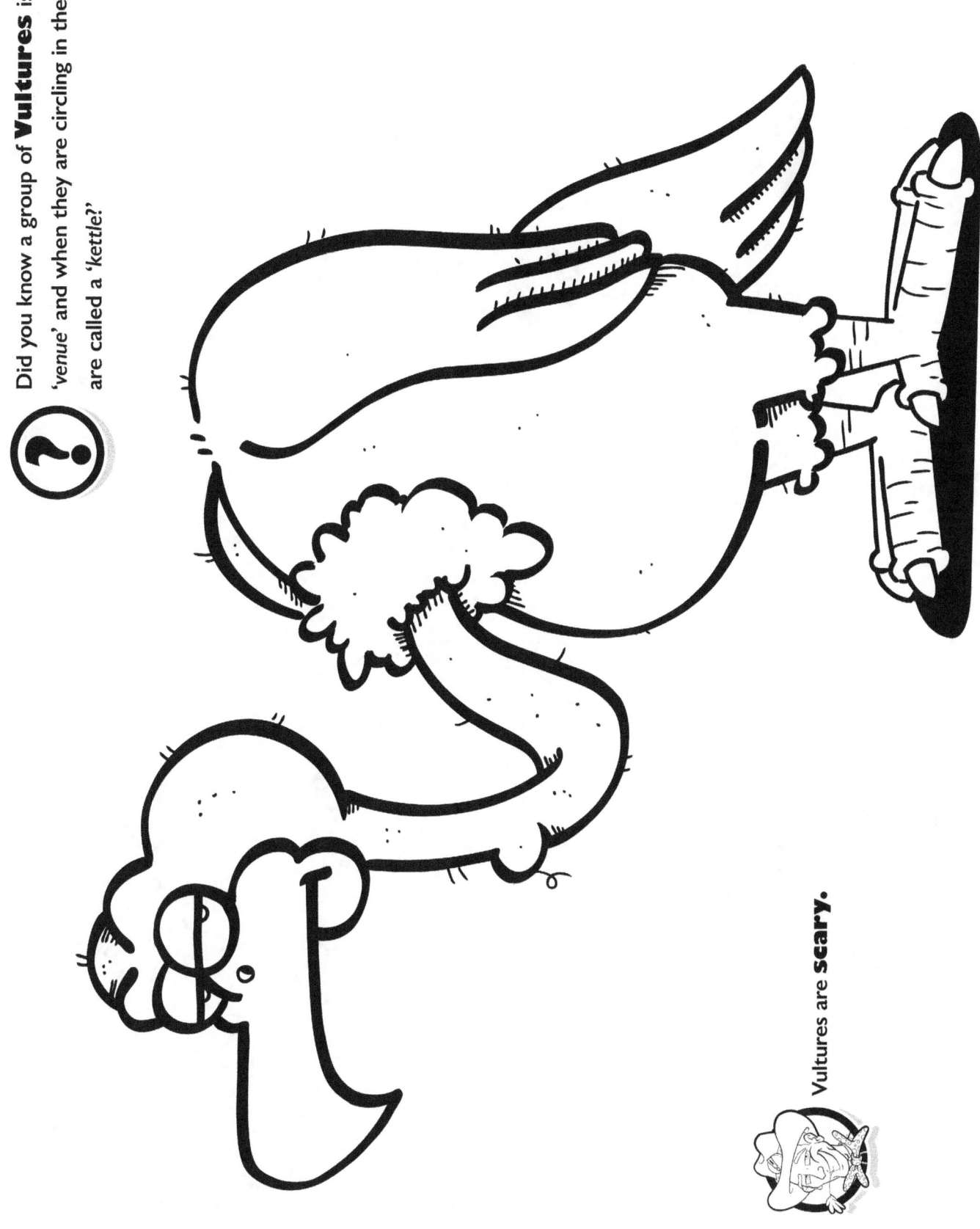

Vultures are **scary.**

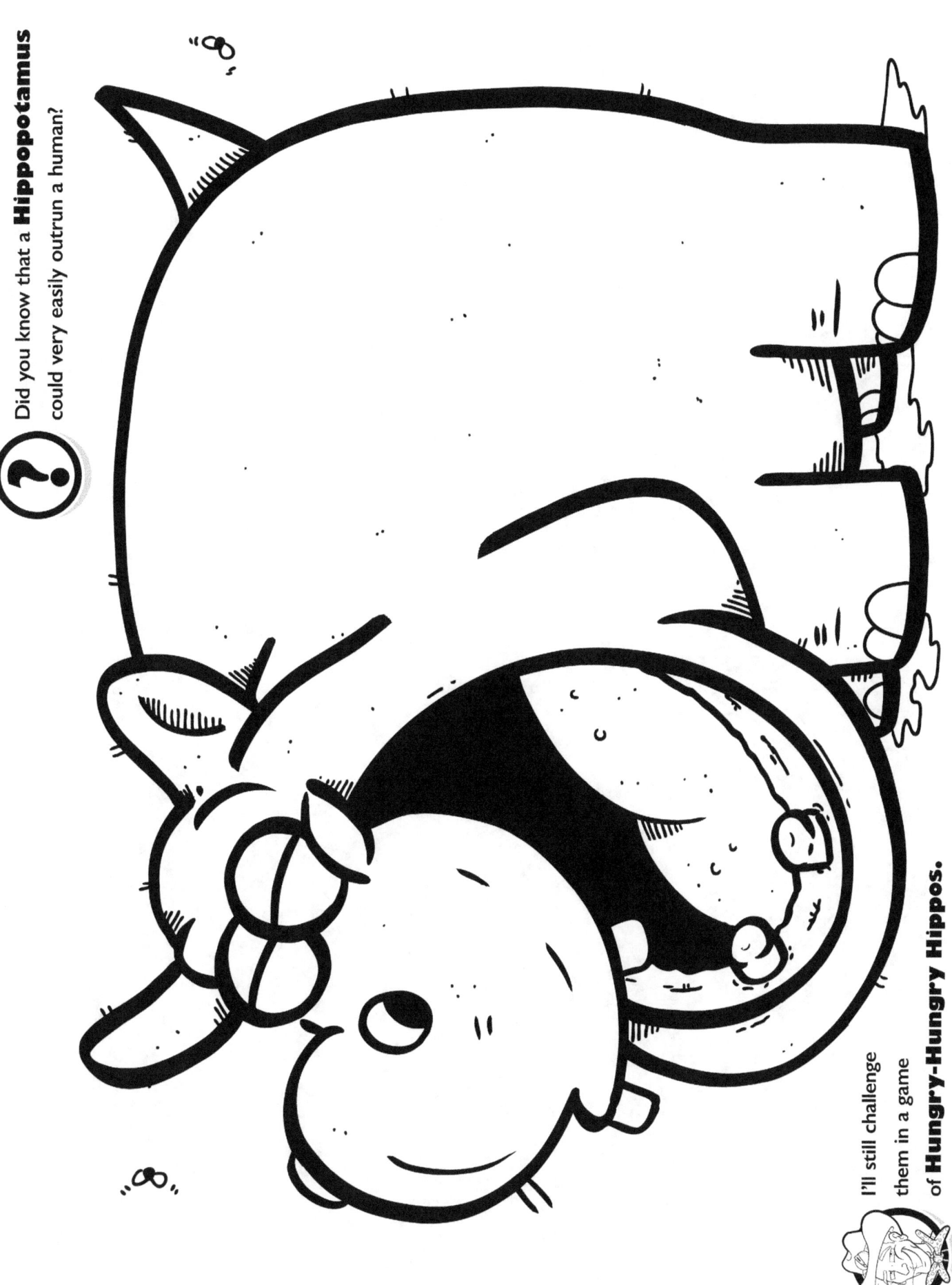

? Did you know that a **Hippopotamus** could very easily outrun a human?

I'll still challenge them in a game of **Hungry-Hungry Hippos.**

Did you know the first Olympic mascot was a **Wiener Dog?**

His name was **Waldi.**

? Did you know that every **Zebra** has a distinct pattern of stripes?

Remember to use your Imagination. A zebra can be any color you want it to be.

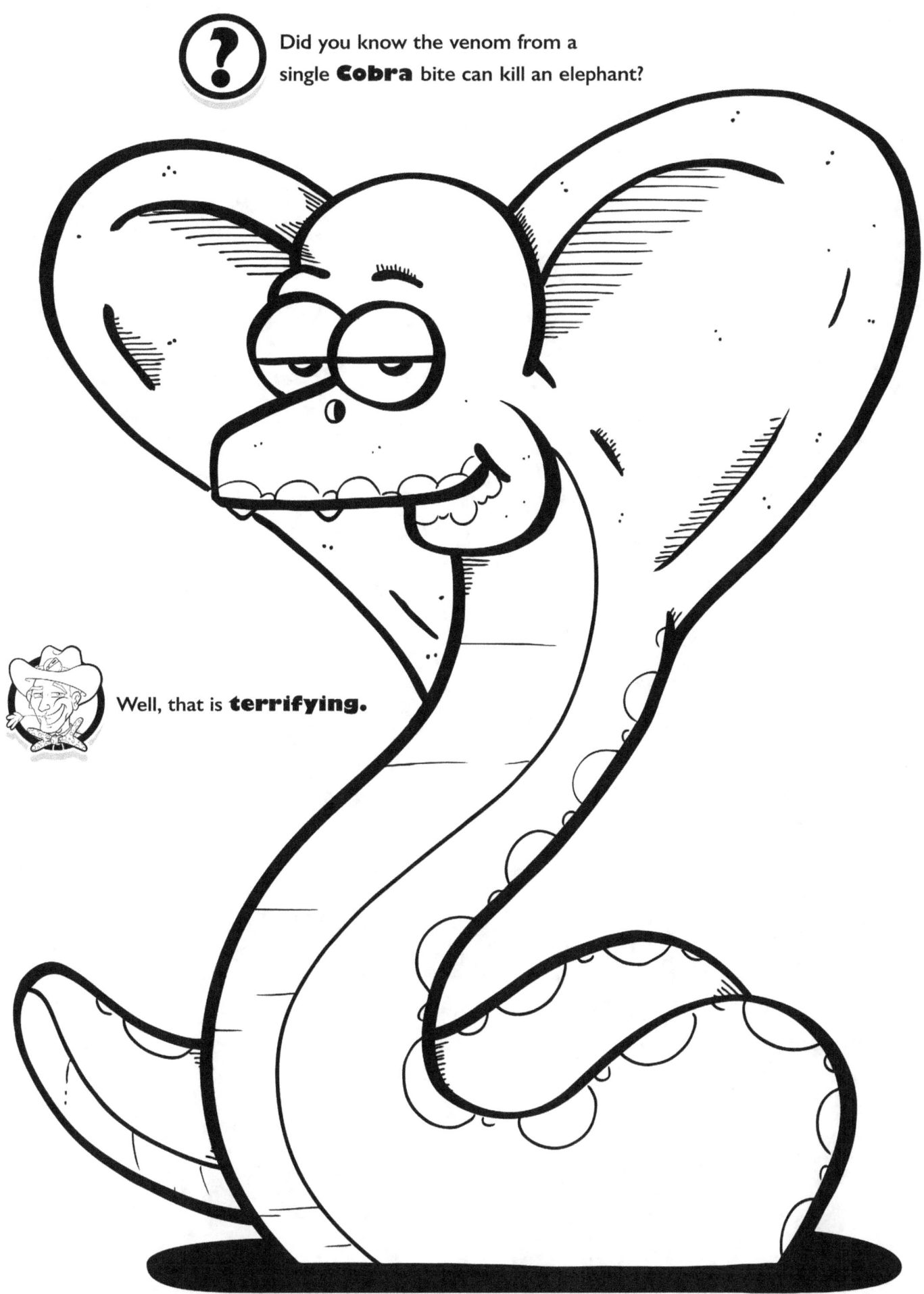

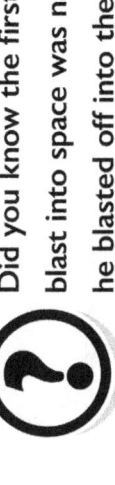

Did you know the first **Space Monkey** to blast into space was named Albert? On June 11, 1948 he blasted off into the stars on a v2 rocket.

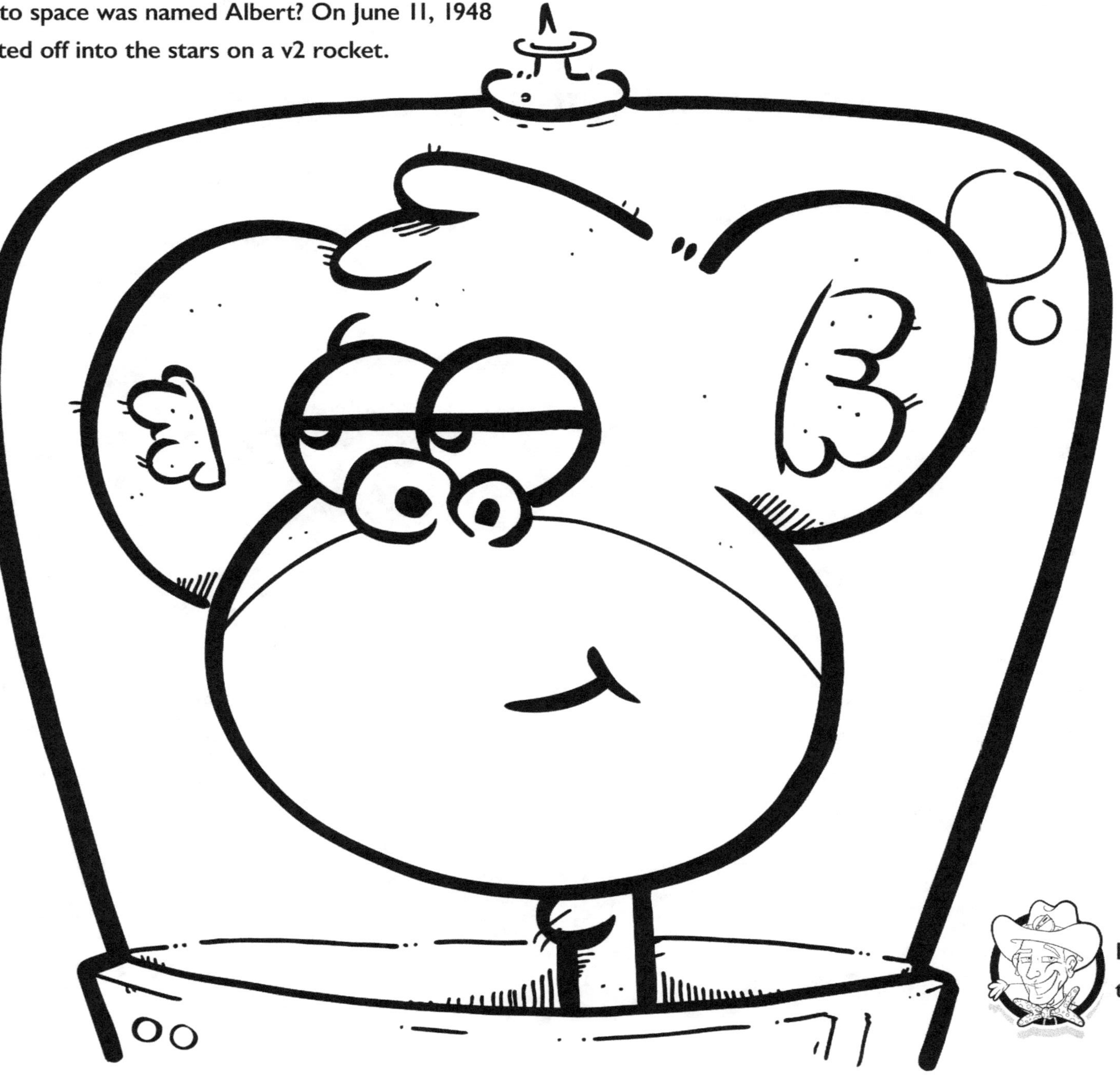

I bet monkeys make the best **co-pilots**.

? Did you know **Wild Turkeys** are able to fly up to 55 mph?

Something tells me this turkey enjoys **strutting** instead of flying.

 Did you know **Octopuses** have three hearts? Two that pump the blood through the gills and the third pumps blood to the rest of the body.

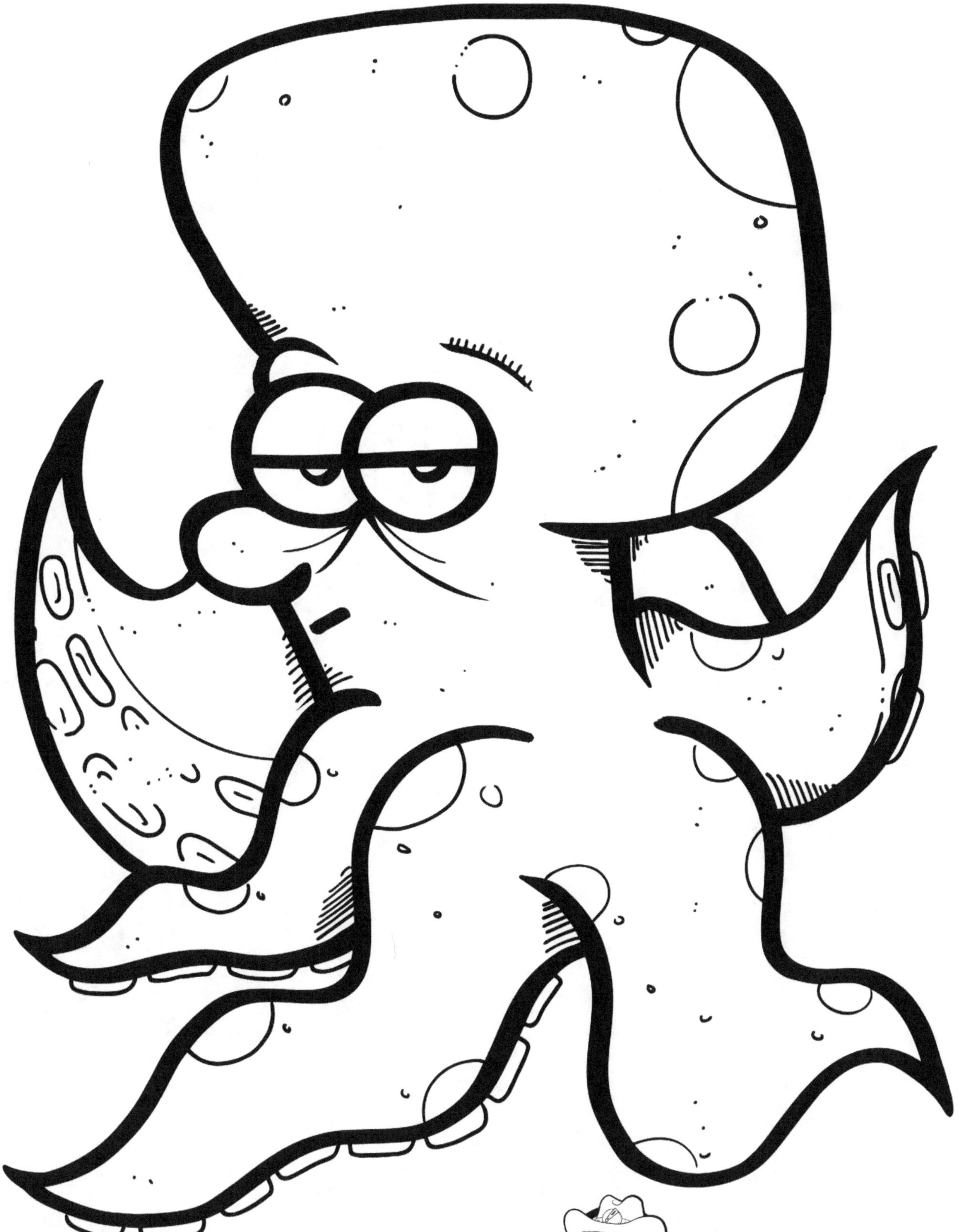

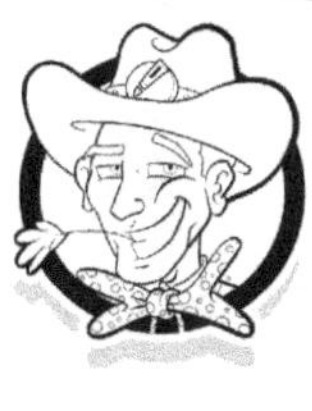

They must be really **caring** with those three hearts.

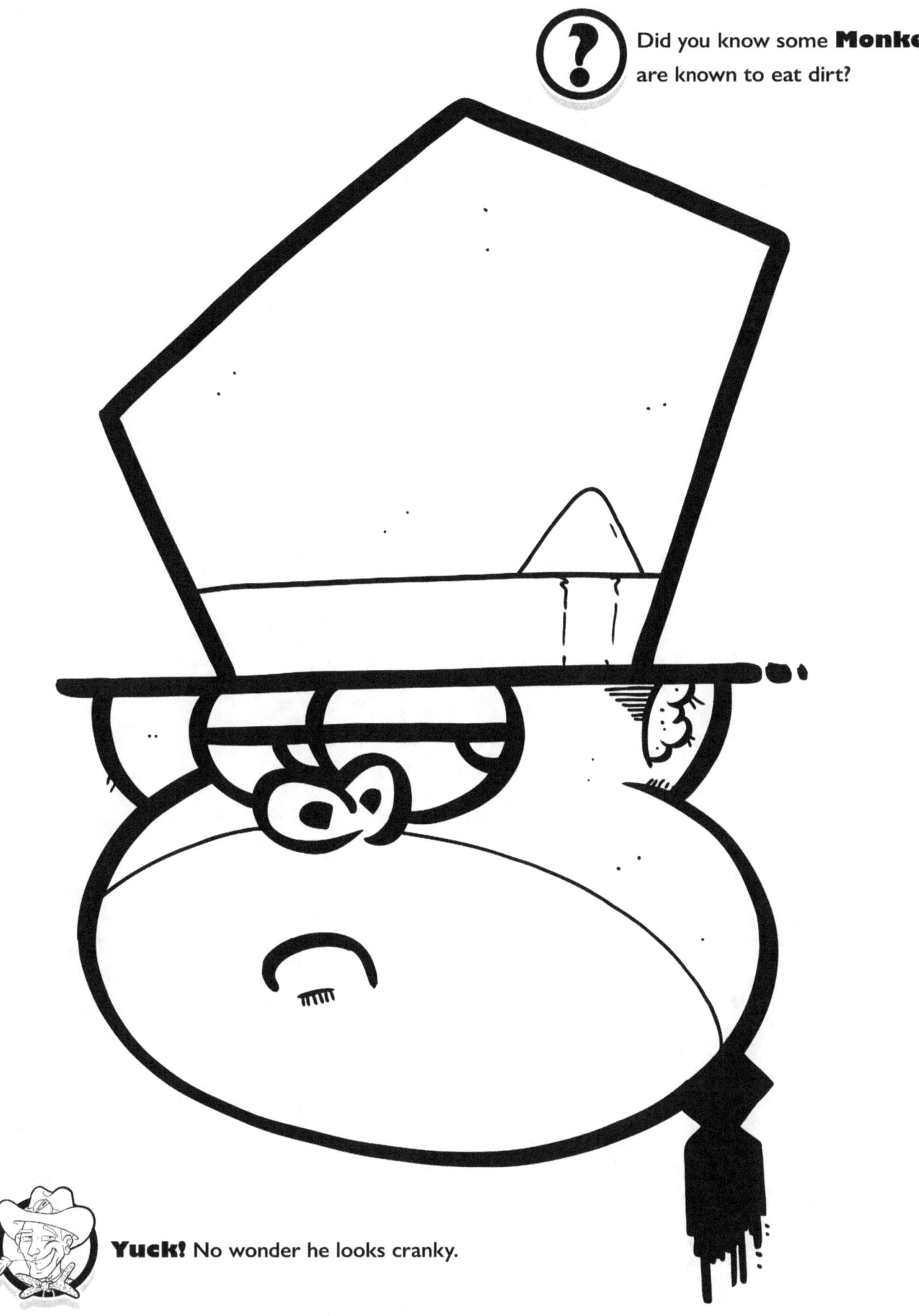

Did you know some **Monkeys** are known to eat dirt?

Yuck! No wonder he looks cranky.

? Did you know a male **Donkey** is called a Jack and a female donkey is called a Jenny?

If I owned a donkey farm I'd name it **Jack & Jenny.**

 Did you know a **Llama's** foot has only two toenails?

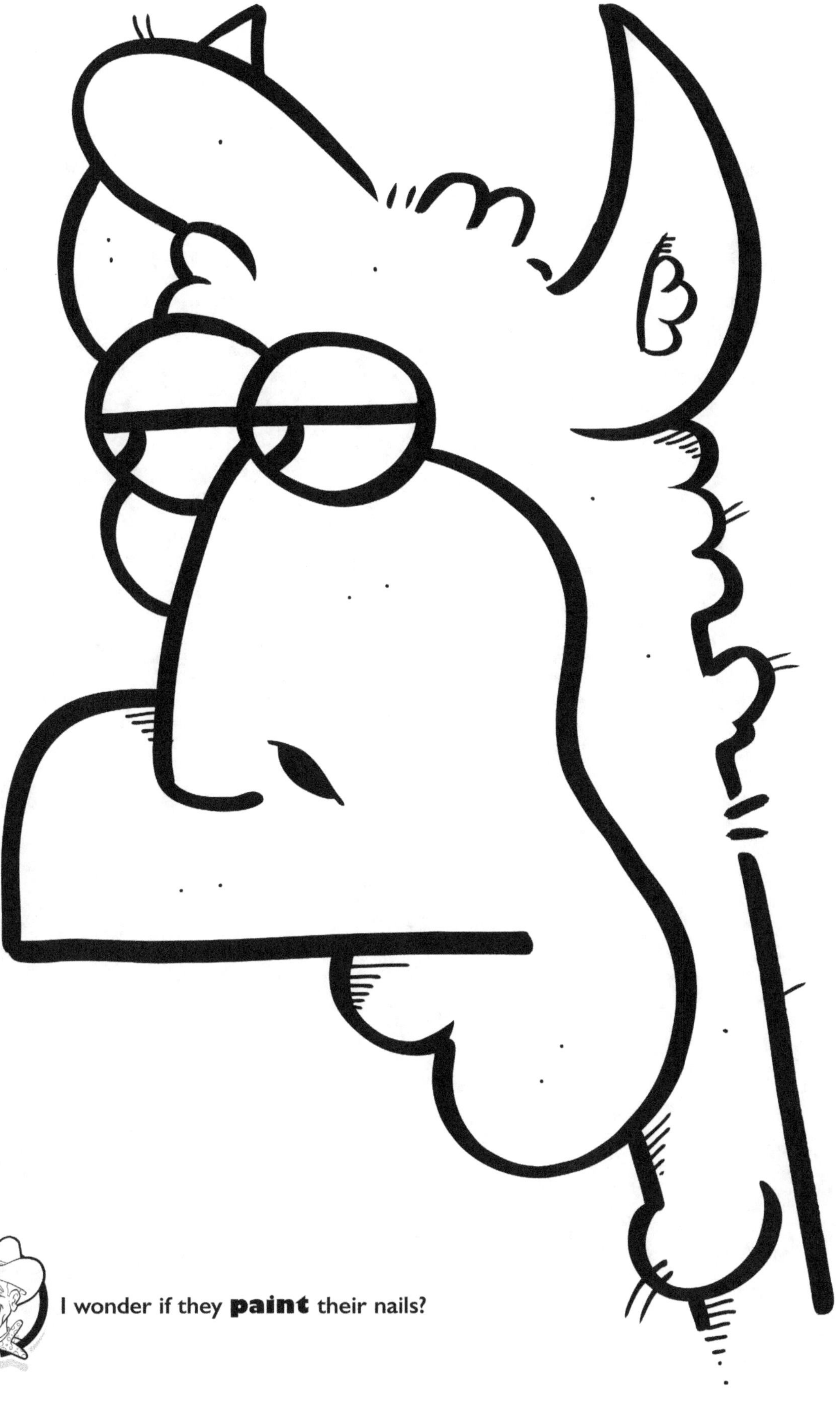

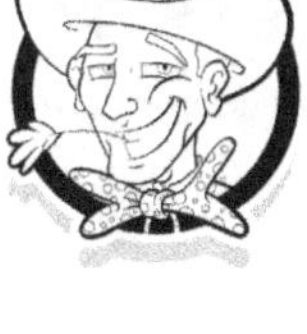

I wonder if they **paint** their nails?

 Did you know the gut of a **Panda** is covered in a thick layer of mucus to protect it against splinters from the bamboo?

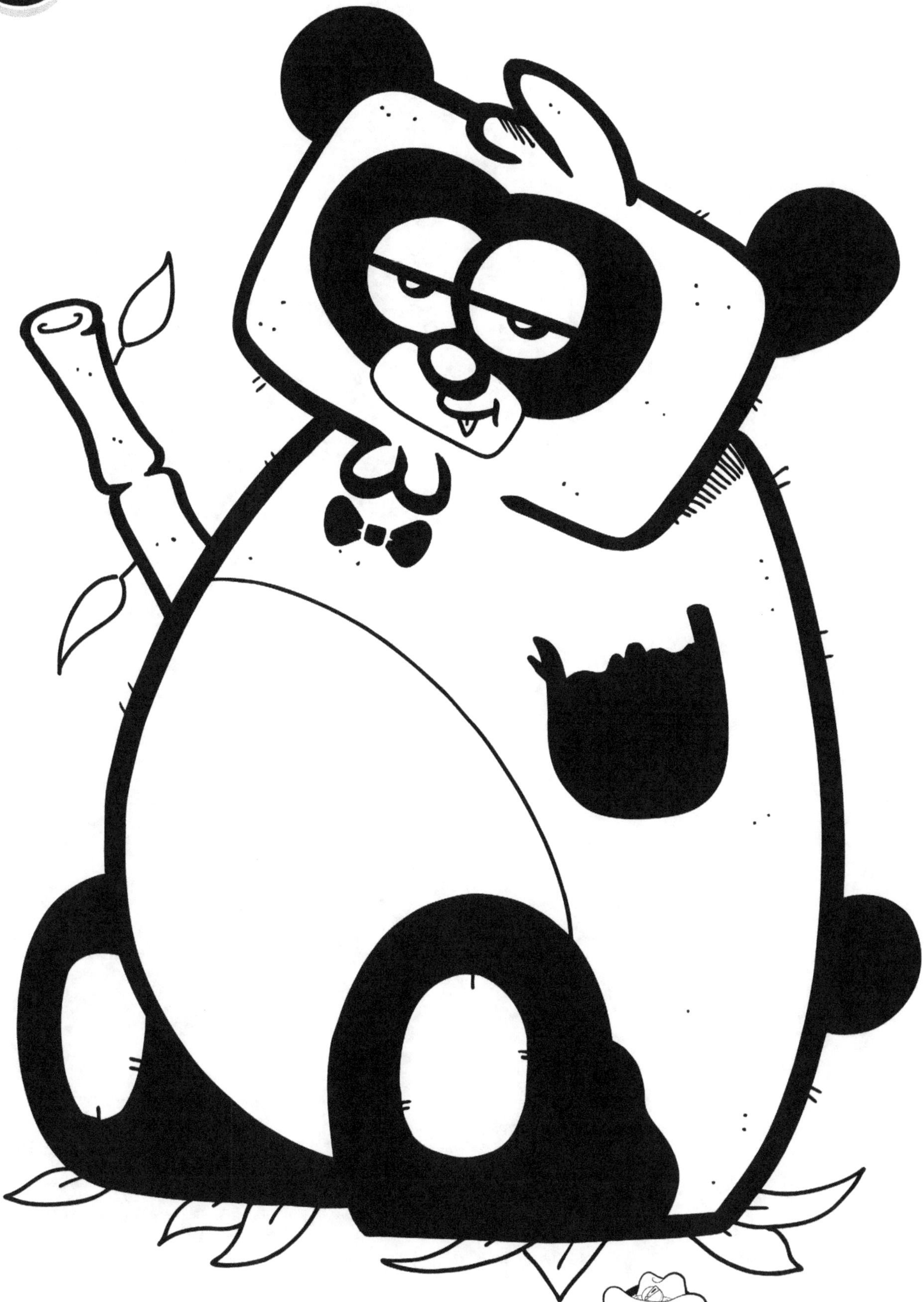

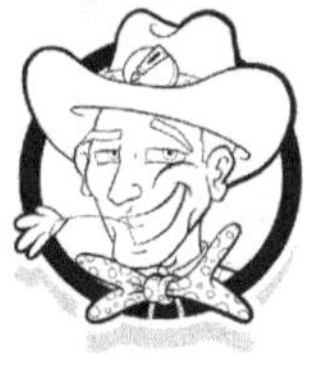

Why don't they just eat **ice cream** instead?

Did you know **Elephants** are the world's largest land animals?

I've **always** wanted to ride around on an elephant.

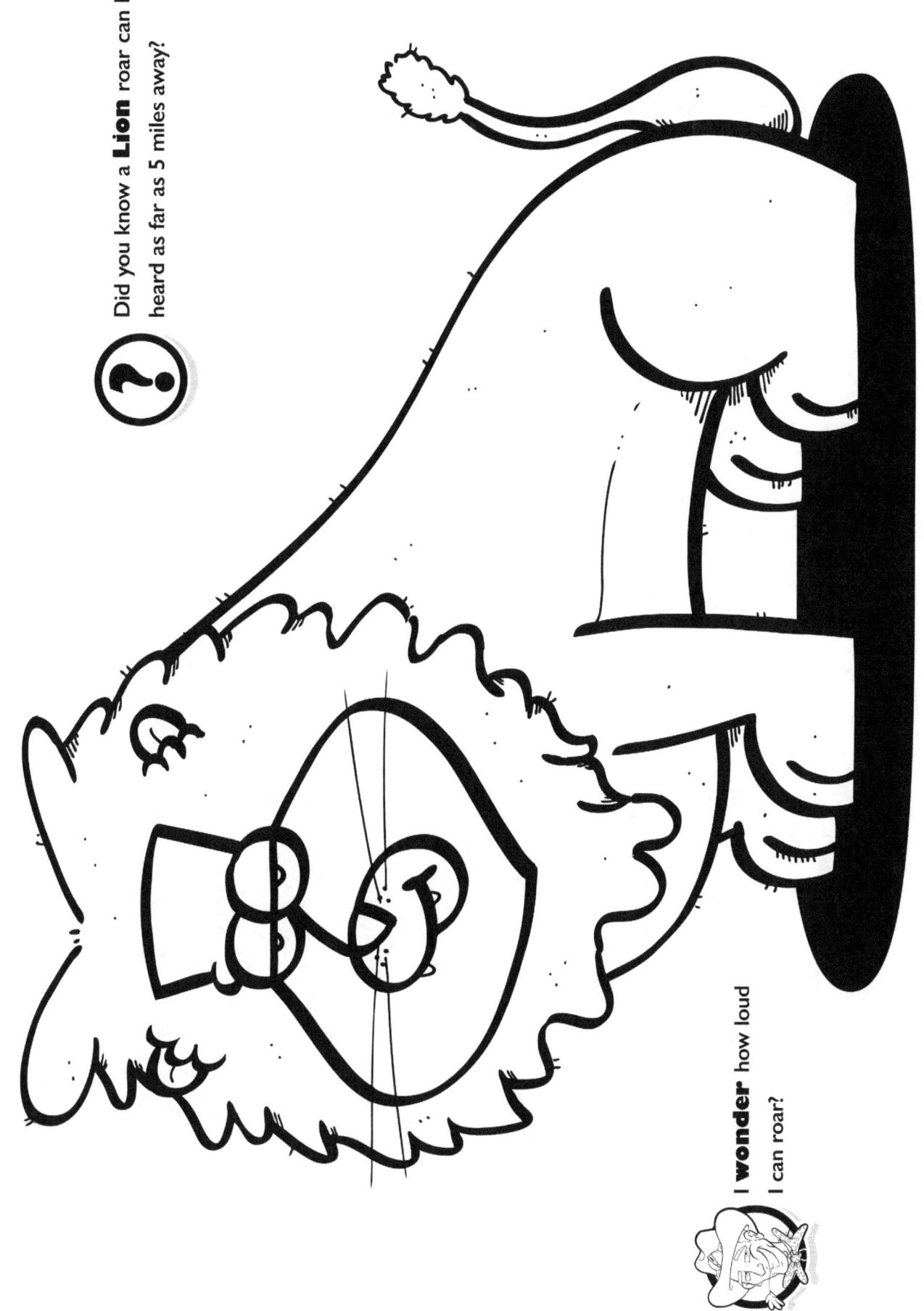

Did you know a **Lion** roar can be heard as far as 5 miles away?

I **wonder** how loud I can roar?

Did you know a male **Deer** grows new antlers every year?

If I had antlers I would hang funny **lights** from them.

? Did you know **Seagulls** can drink both fresh *and* salt water?

Yeah, they also **love** to eat and drink my food when I'm at the beach!

? Did you know **Clownfish** are actually naturally aggressive fish?

I don't think this clownfish even knows he's **aggressive.**

? Did you know, depending on the species, some **Frogs** can leap between 3 and 7 feet?

I bet they're really good at **leapfrog.**

? Did you know the average garden **Snail** travels at the speed of 50 yards per hour?

Mmmm... **tatsy** snail.

Did you know the name **Rhinoceros** has Greek origins meaning *'nose horn?'*

I mean, talk about **literal.**

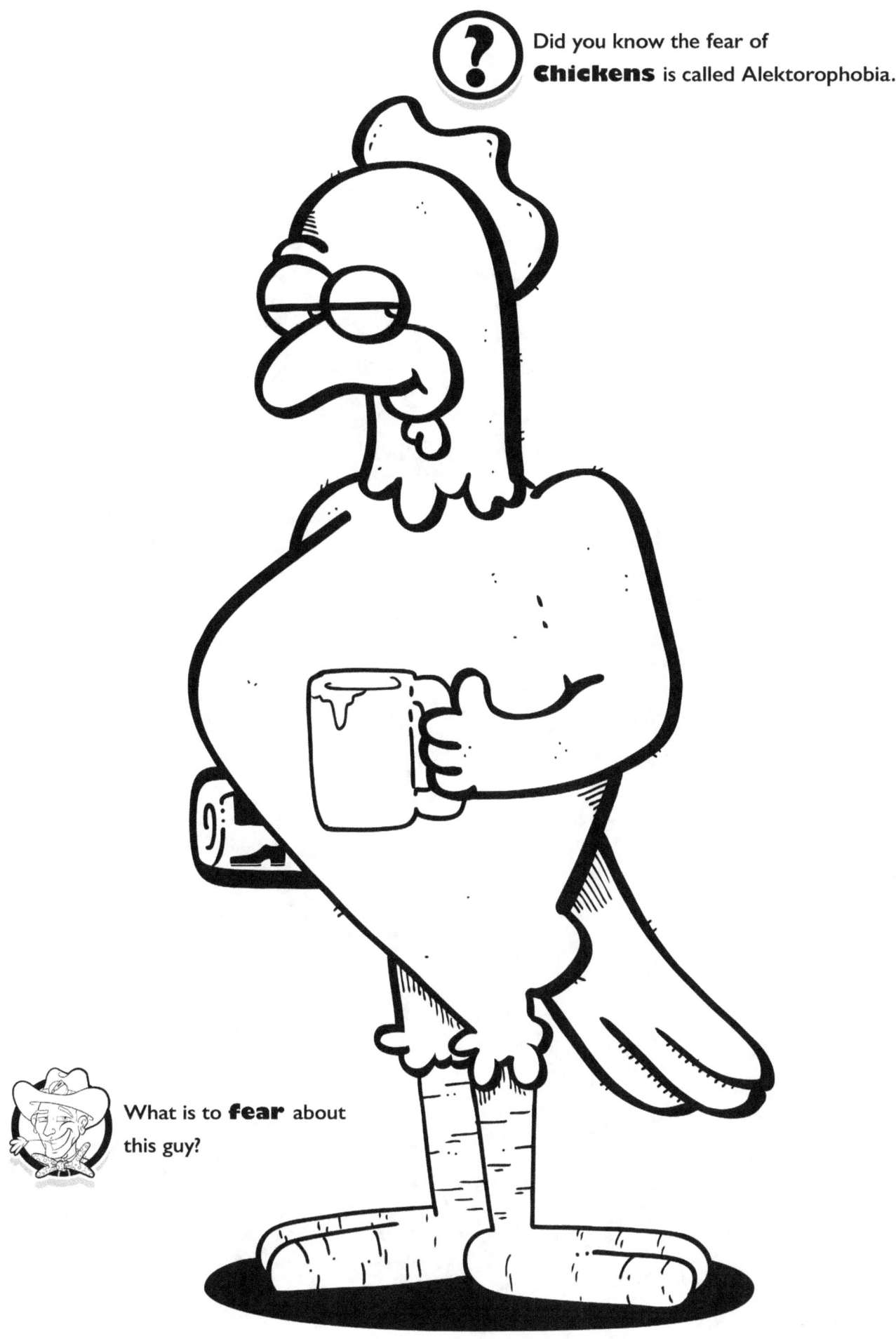

? Did you know a **Cow** doesn't actually bite grass? They use their tongue to rip it out of the ground instead.

Didn't a cow **jump** over the moon one time?

? Did you know **Mice** eat about 15-20 times a day?

No wonder they keep taking my **cheese!**

? Do you know one thing that can make **Monkeys** even cooler? Hawaiian shirts.

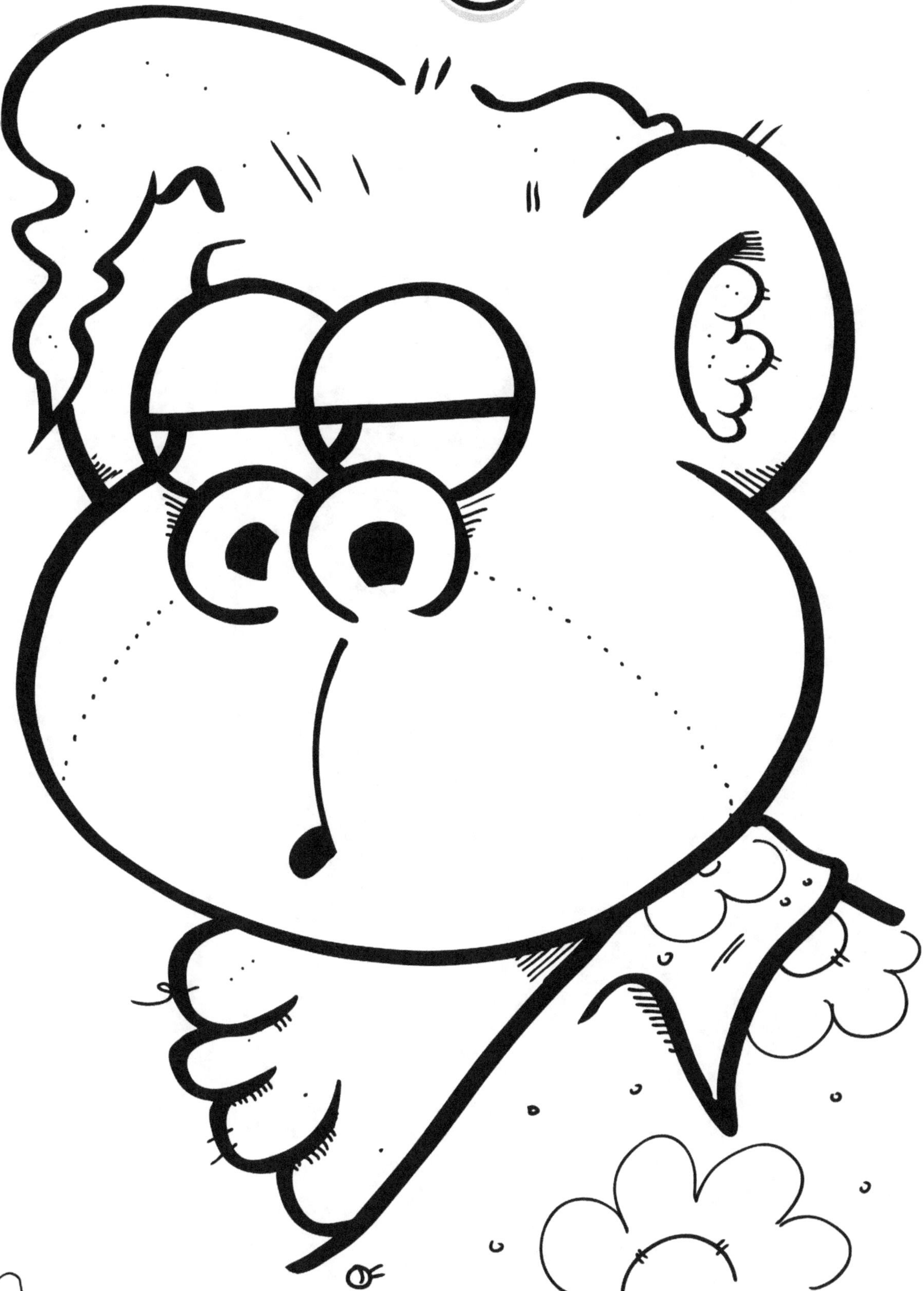

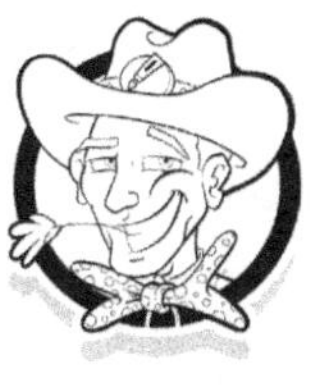

Cool **shirt** monkey man.

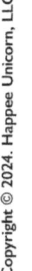

? Did you know a **Starfish** does not have a brain or even blood?

Do they make a wish when they see a **shooting star?**

Pencil - Pirate Parrot

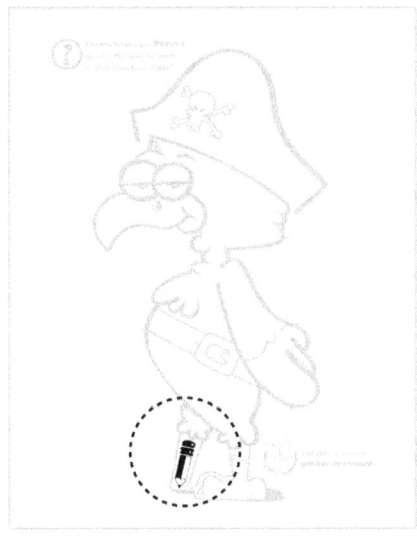

Inside Wooden Leg

Briefcase - Mariachi Fly

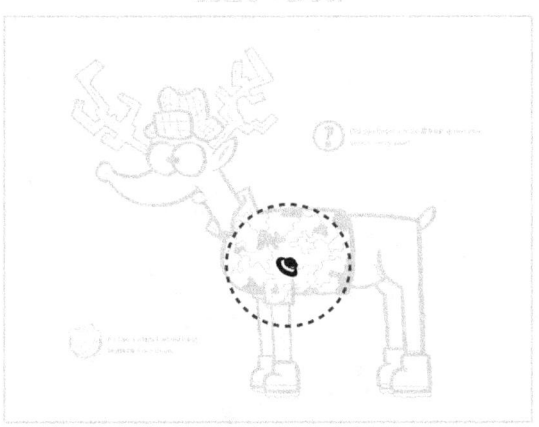

On Top Of Hat

Watch - Rat

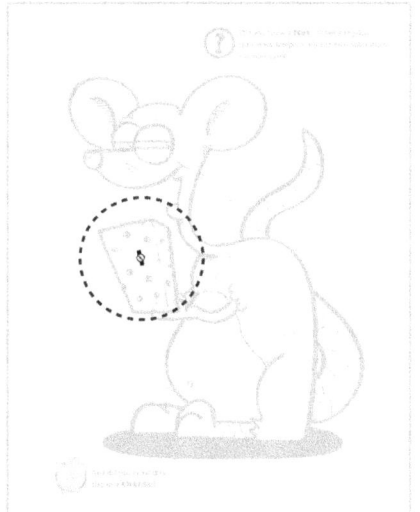

Inside Cheese

Marker - Mechanical Bulldog

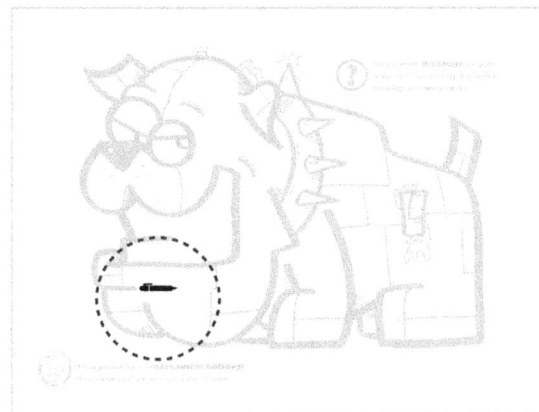

On Bottom Lip

Mr. Gray's
Hidden Treasure
Answer Sheet

Coffee - Sloth

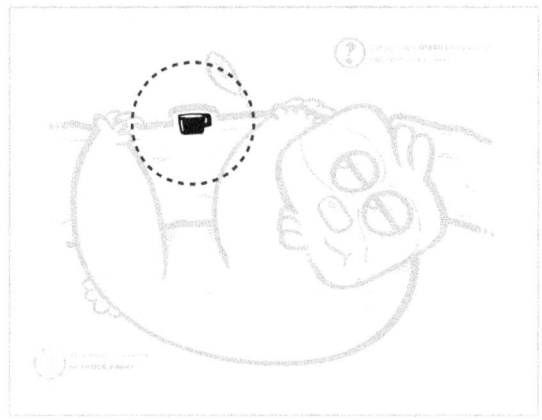

Inside Tree Branch

Bow Tie - Panda

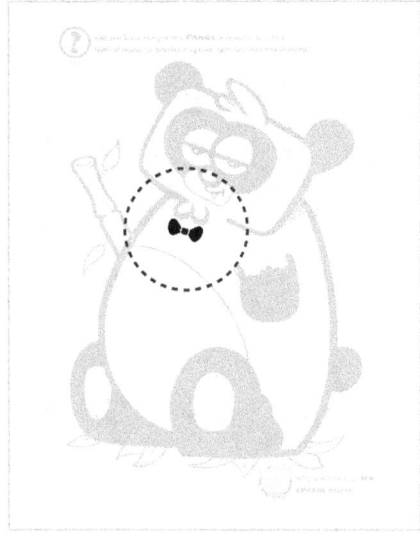

On Top Of Chest

Hat - Deer

Inside Camouflage

Shoe - Chicken

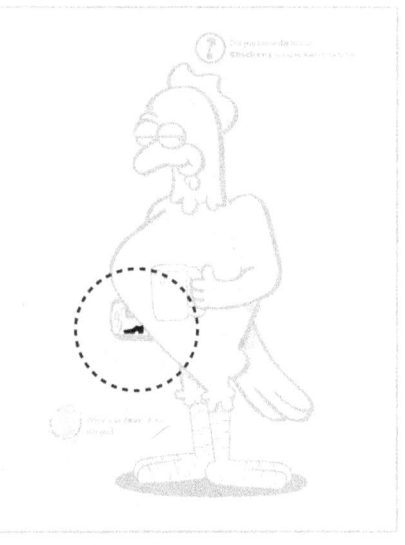

On Newspaper

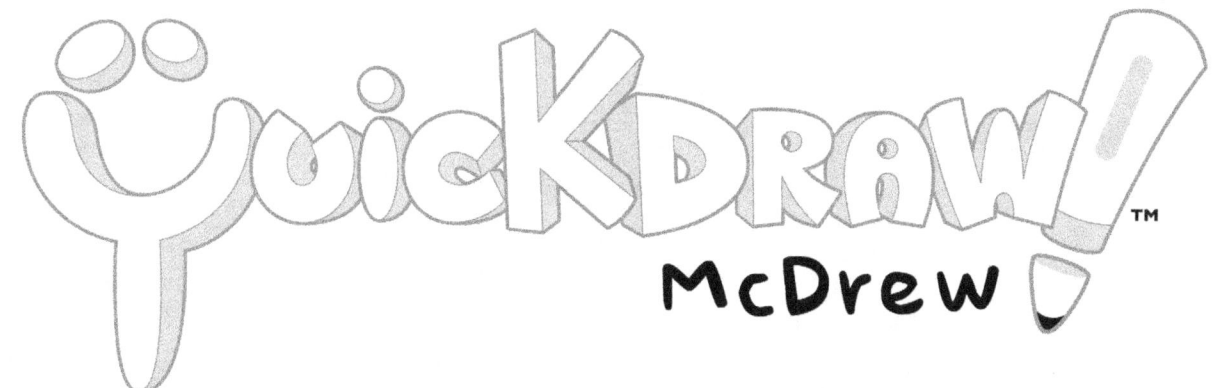

McDrew

Howdy! My name is Mr. Gray, a.k.a. QuickDraw McDrew! The Fastest Cartoon Slinger in the West!™ I'm on a mission to awaken and strengthen the imagination that lives in all of us, because the truth is, imagination never truly dies. It just likes to play hide-n-seek from time to time, but I promise you it's still there. Like a baby riding a unicorn flying through space shooting planets with a booger gun! *(See, it's alive and well and we just need to find it.)* And together we will!

Your Wascally Cartoonist,

Mr. Gray

-Mr.G

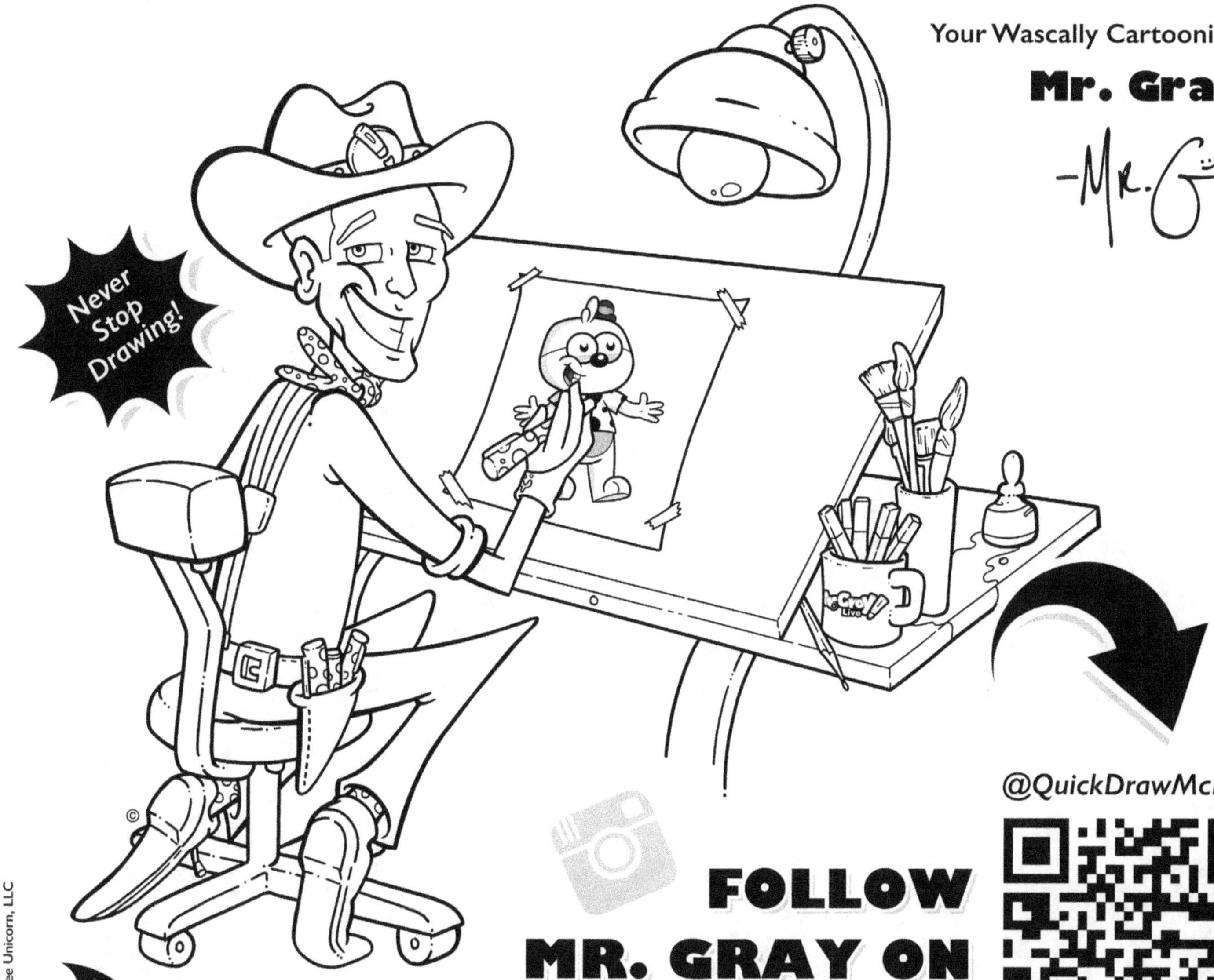

Never Stop Drawing!

Write Mr. Gray:
Mr. Gray
P.O. Box 11711
Burbank, CA 91510

QuickDrawMcDrew.com

@QuickDrawMcDrew

FOLLOW MR. GRAY ON INSTAGRAM

COLLECT THEM ALL!

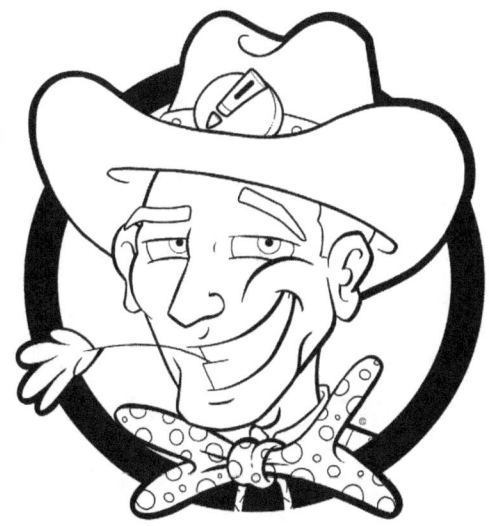

amazon.com
Prime

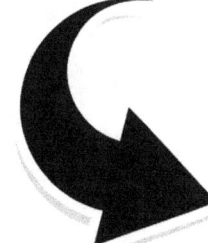

The
ANIMALS & FRIENDS

Coloring Book | Volume Two

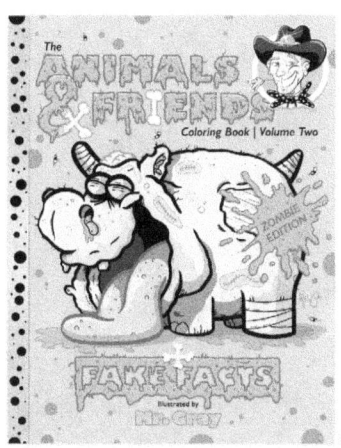

Mr. Gray's
ANIMAL MASH UP!

Coloring Book | Volume One

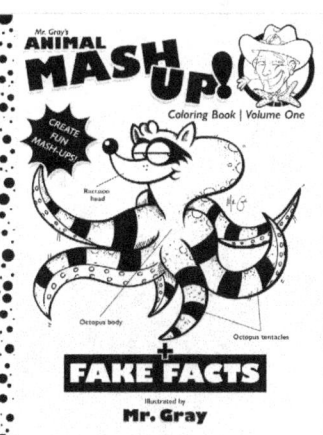

The
SUPER FANTASTICAL FLAVOR-FILLED FOOD

Coloring Book | Volume One

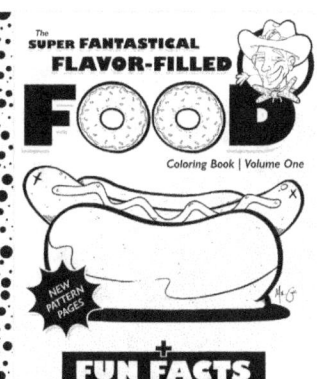

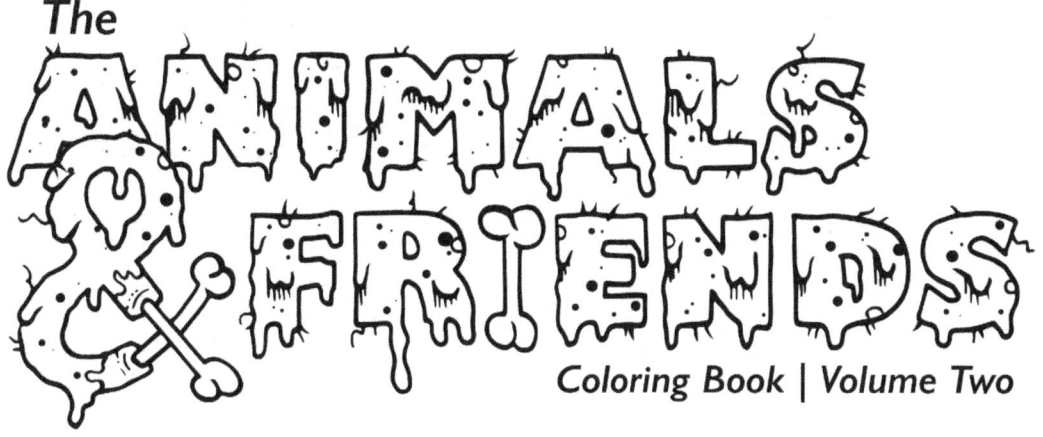

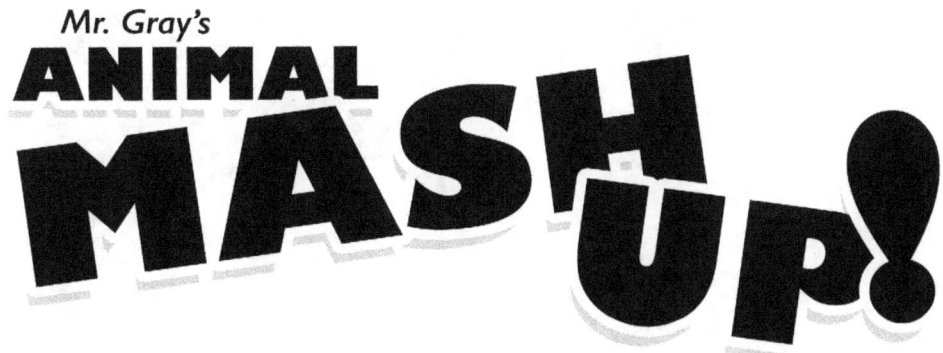

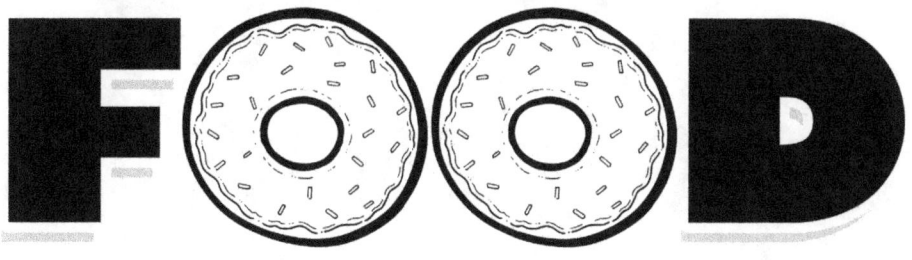

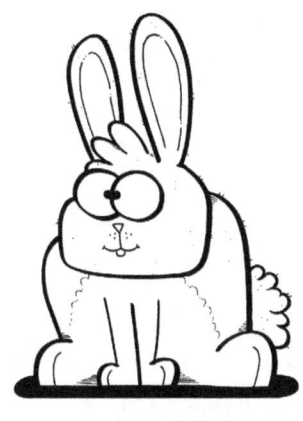

THE END

ISBN: 978-0-9988005-0-9

Third Edition. Printed by Amazon in the United States of America

Happee Unicorn, LLC - P.O. Box 11711, Burbank, CA 91510

Business Inquiries: mrgray@mrgrayart.com

www.mrgrayart.com

www.ingramcontent.com/pod-product-compliance
Lightning Source LLC
Chambersburg PA
CBHW080959170526

45158CB00010B/2846